"Hope is the First Great Blessing"

LEAVES FROM THE AFRICAN FREE SCHOOL PRESENTATION BOOK

1812–1826

"Hope is the First Great Blessing"

LEAVES FROM THE AFRICAN FREE SCHOOL PRESENTATION BOOK

1812–1826

By David W. Blight, Anna Mae Duane, James O. Horton, and Thomas Thurston

WITH AN INTRODUCTORY NOTE BY Jean Ashton

AND A PREFACE BY Louise Mirrer

THE NEW-YORK HISTORICAL SOCIETY

2008

ISBN 10: 0916141217

ISBN 13: 9780916141219

Table of Contents

Preface

Two hundred and twenty years ago, members of the New-York Manumission Society founded a school in New York, which graduated some of the most remarkable figures in American history: James McCune Smith, the nation's first black physician; Charles Reason, who became a professor of Greek, Latin, mathematics and natural philosophy; future abolitionist leaders Henry Highland Garnet and Alexander Crummell; George T. Downing, the restaurant owner and reformer; the actor, Ira Aldridge; and Samuel Ringgold Ward, one of the greatest black orators of his time. For a city in which one out of every five persons was enslaved, the school's founding mission in 1787 was nearly unprecedented: the African Free School sought to educate black children.

The New-York Historical Society is extremely fortunate—and proud—to hold within its Library collection the papers of the New-York Manumission Society, and of the African Free School. For the past three years, these papers have been showcased in three major exhibitions: *Alexander Hamilton*; *Slavery in New York*; and *New York Divided: Slavery and the Civil War*. In the near future, the papers of the African Free School will again play a role in the Society's exhibition program as the dynamic relationship among the American, French and Haitian revolutions is explored. Visitors to this new exhibition will have a chance to view the extraordinary proclamation written by eleven-year old McCune Smith and presented to the Marquis de Lafayette, who visited the School in 1824.

The papers of the New-York Manumission Society and the African Free School are of clear significance to those who have studied and written about early American history. And yet they have never been edited, and they have never, before this facsimile edition, been made available as a publication. This astonishing fact was brought to my attention shortly after I became president of the Society in 2004, and I vowed that the editing and publication of the papers of the African Free School—a more manageable project than the entire New-York Manumission Society records—would be a priority.

I am grateful to Eric Wanner and the Russell Sage Foundation for recognizing the importance of this project from the start, and for providing a grant that allowed us to set it in motion. We have, in addition, received generous funding for the publication from the Department of Education's Underground Railroad Educational and Cultural Program.

Finally, I would like to thank David Blight, a Society trustee, for generously sharing his knowledge of James McCune Smith; and James Oliver Horton and Lois Horton, whose work on American slavery has been an inspiration for the Society's eighteen-month initiative on slavery in New York. Jean Ashton, the Society's Library Director, is truly responsible for the project's success. Her intelligence, dynamic leadership, and deep understanding of the Library collection are unparalleled. I treasure her colleagueship.

The New-York Historical Society holds many, many unedited works of signal importance to understanding the history of the United States. It is my hope that these works will soon join the publications initiative begun with this project.

LOUISE MIRRER
President and CEO, The New-York Historical Society

Introductory Note

The New-York Historical Society was founded in 1804, with the explicit mission "to discover, procure, and preserve whatever may relate to the natural, civil, literary, and ecclesiastical history of the United States." Its founders, some of whom were also founding members of the New-York Manumission Society, the parent body of the African Free School, took seriously their task of collecting the basic documents of the recent past. Since many of them had lived through the struggle to separate the American colonies from their English rulers, and to establish a republican government capable of protecting their perceived liberties, the difficulty of establishing new institutions that could benefit from the practices of the past without repeating its devastating errors was still fresh among them. Their vision, set out clearly in an initial address to the public in February of their first year, asserted their intent to go about "the humble task of collecting and preserving whatever may be useful to others in the different branches of historical inquiry," thus supporting their conviction that "without the aid of original records and authentic documents, history will be nothing more than a well-combined series of ingenious conjectures and amusing fables."

The success of these efforts and those of the founders' descendents and fellow citizens is reflected in the rich and varied trove of primary resources that form the New-York Historical Society's collections. Among these are the papers drawn upon for this publication, the records of the New-York Society for Promoting the Manumission of Slaves and Protecting Such of Them as Have Been or May Be Liberated, and the associated papers of the African Free School, which the Manumission Society founded in 1787.

The eleven volumes of records of the Manumission Society are comprised of minutes of the quarterly meetings of the group from 1785 until its dissolution in 1849, account books, registers of manumissions, indentures, and reports. Along with four additional volumes pertaining to the African Free School, including the examination papers reproduced here, the documents reflect the concern of the early citizens of the new republic with the problems inherent in accommodating a system of involuntary servitude within a nation that had based its rebellion against England on a demand for liberty. The founders of the Manumission Society, observing in their earliest statements that all men had been given an equal right to life, liberty and property by their "benevolent Creator," pledged themselves to endeavor to provide such benefits to those unjustly held in servitude and to protect those among the freed population who were vulnerable and in need of help. Although they included slaveholders as well as fierce proponents of abolition, the members actively supported the elimination of the international slave trade, encouraged the liberation of individual slaves, urged the enforcement of laws banning the sale of slaves in New York State, and provided funds for the legal defense of fugitives and escapees, as well as free African Americans who found themselves subject to kidnapping and violence. The decision to establish a school to remedy the ill effects of legal oppression and the debates around its nature and function are recorded in detail in the minute books of the Society, which are then complemented by the documents surrounding the growth and progress of school itself. Together, as the introductory essays point out, the fifteen volumes form a unique resource for further study, as well as an unusually vivid glimpse into the lives of a group of important New Yorkers.

Documenting the past is never a straightforward task. The Library collections were drawn on heavily for the two exhibitions at The New-York Historical Society that have opened the way for an exploration of the emotionally freighted subject of slavery in the city and state, *Slavery in New York* (2005-06) and *New York Divided: Slavery and the Civil War* (2006-07). Like the African Free School volumes, the printed and manuscript materials underlying such an exploration—maps, letters, diaries, indentures, contracts, broadsides, and newspapers—enabled scholars to understand the contexts of social and political struggle, to envision the physical and geographical features that had an impact on daily lives, and to examine in detail the cultural and political communities in which New Yorkers lived their sometimes brief and painful lives. By publishing and editing this edition of the Presentation book, we hope to extend to a broader public a similar opportunity to look at (and enjoy) one of those authentic documents that our founders hoped would combat the ingenious conjectures that underlie our national myth.

JEAN W. ASHTON
Executive Vice President; Director of the Library, The New-York Historical Society

James McCune Smith and The African Free Schools

The ideal of national independence and the language of individual freedom that animated the American Revolution formed the context for the heated debates on the continued presence of slavery in the new nation. In northern states, where slavery was generally less powerful than in the South, many, taking the words of the Declaration to heart, organized to bring freedom to those who remained in bondage. Some of New York's most influential men came together to found The New-York Manumission Society in 1785. Among them were such luminaries as Alexander Hamilton and first Chief Justice of the Supreme Court, John Jay. They hoped to end slavery in the city and state, but they would go further in assisting the former slaves in their transition to freedom. The African Free School, begun by the Manumission Society in 1787, was an important step in that direction.

The African Free School was not the first educational effort focusing on African Americans undertaken in New York. As early as 1704 English missionaries, working through the Society for the Propagation of the Gospel in Foreign Parts, opened a school offering religious education as a means of preparing its black students, most of whom were slaves, for baptism. Society officials argued that educated Africans would make better workers and convinced many slave masters to allow their slaves to attend. Despite the best efforts of dedicated teachers like Ellis Neau, a young French-born evangelist, instruction was difficult, hampered by the demands that slavery made upon exhausted students. Still, in these schools, hundreds of Africans, some only recently arrived in New York, learned to read and write English.[1]

Many slaveholders, however, remained suspicious of these schools, fearing that education might encourage dissatisfaction and resistance among slaves. They fantasized about contented slaves happy to do their master's bidding, but had nightmares about rebellious slaves like those who had burned parts of New York City during the uprising of 1712. Particularly alarming was the discovery that two of the rebels were Ellis Neau's students. That discovery brought black education in the city to a temporary halt.

By 1750, antislavery Quaker Anthony Benezet had begun a school for blacks in Philadelphia, while Catholic clergyman Thomas Bacon started one in Frederick County, Maryland. By the time the New York African Free School was established at the end of the 18th century, then, African schools—while not common—were at least not unknown.

Over the next three generations, black education expanded in the North. In 1789 Primus Hall, a free black man in Boston, opened a school to educate the city's blacks. Former slaves George Bell, Nicholas Franklin, and Moses Liverpool opened the Bell school in Washington D.C. in 1807, and three years later a British woman, Mary Billings, opened another black school in neighboring Georgetown. In some places in New England, New York, Pennsylvania, and in a few Midwestern states, public schools were opened to blacks. For the most part, however, they were relegated to underfunded segregated public schools or inferior private schools.[2]

By the 1820s a second black school, the African Free School No. 2, had been opened on New York City's Mulberry Street. A boys' school accommodating five hundred students, enrollment continued to expand to a roster of 1,400 students in the 1830s. In order to accommodate rising numbers, the Public School Society then took over from the Manumission Society, and four additional schools were added.³

Meanwhile, the education of slaves had become illegal in most Southern states, especially in the wake of several slave conspiracies and rebellions led by literate blacks. Chief among these were Gabriel's rebellion in 1800 in Richmond, Virginia; Denmark Vesey's 1822 conspiracy in Charleston, South Carolina; and the most notorious slave revolt of all, led by Virginia slave Nat Turner in 1831. Increasingly, Southern whites viewed the education of African Americans as dangerous, and they passed laws with stiff penalties to prevent it.

Their concerns were ultimately valid. It was the most educated African Americans who generally posed the greatest threat to slavery, and many of those educated at New York's African Free School provided striking examples. From its earliest years, the school encouraged antislavery ideas and self confidence. Teachers taught the students that they "had as much capacity to acquire knowledge as any other children." Classes promoted public oratory skills, and at special events the rhetoric of abolitionism was ubiquitous. Many recalled that the students were proud of their accomplishments and outspoken in their beliefs. "Freedom will break the tyrant's chains," predicted twelve-year-old Thomas Sidney in his poem of 1828. He and his classmates grew to be some of the most powerful future abolitionist leaders in the country.⁴

Among the group was Henry Highland Garnet, whose father, a former African chief, escaped from slavery in Maryland with his family in 1821. After his time at the African Free School, Garnet went on to become one of the most effective abolitionist speakers in the nation. In 1843, he delivered a powerful address to a convention of African Americans in Buffalo calling for organized slave rebellion. Alexander Crummell, who went on to graduate from Cambridge University in England and become an Episcopal minister, writer and abolitionist speaker, was also in Sidney's class. So was Charles Reason, one of the most effective voices of abolition in America, England and the Caribbean.

As young boys, ages thirteen to sixteen, these students formed themselves into an abolitionist society. "For years," one remembered, "our society met on [the Fourth of July], and the time was devoted to planning schemes for the freeing and upbuilding of our race." Young Garnet, it was said, led the group in their vow that after their education they would, "go South, start an insurrection and free our brethren in bondage."⁵

Other African Free School graduates included George T. Downing, restaurant owner and reformer, Ira Aldridge, a celebrated actor known in Europe as well as the United States, Samuel Ringgold Ward, considered by some the greatest black orator of his time, and James McCune Smith, who became a celebrated and influential doctor, educator, reformer, and essayist.

Indeed, it was McCune Smith who embodied the intellectual spirit and educational purpose of the African Free School perhaps more than any other graduate among that extraordinary group in the 1820s. Born in New York City on April 18, 1813, Smith was by his own description, "the son of a slave… and a self-emancipated bond-woman… owing my liberty to the Emancipation Act of the state of New York." He was 14 years old and the star student at Andrews's school when New York officially freed its remaining slaves in 1827. Thirty-eight years later, while writing the introduction for his friend Garnet's *Memorial Discourse*, Smith remembered that special day in 1827 as he now observed a much broader emancipation during the final year of the Civil War. It was "a real full-souled, full-voiced shouting for joy... a proud day, never to be forgotten by young lads who... first felt themselves impelled along that grand procession of liberty, which through perils oft, and dangers oft, through the gloom of midnight, dark and seemingly hopeless," would eventually open into the "joyful light of day."[6]

Clearly, the African Free School provided an environment that allowed the young Smith to imagine a lofty goal—a life of the mind, a career in science and medicine, the chance to write, and to improve upon his an anguished, racist world through words and activism. For a young black student born into slavery, and now in love with learning, art, and language, these were spectacular dreams. He would go on to be the most educated African American of the nineteenth century, but beyond his early New York instruction, he would achieve the rest of his formal education abroad.

Smith's education at the Free School was challenging and thorough for its time. Instruction included spelling, penmanship (at which he excelled, as evidenced in his volume), grammar, geography, and astronomy, with samplings of natural philosophy and navigation. Smith's status as a prize student is demonstrated by the fact that at age 11 he was chosen to deliver a short address on the occasion of the Marquis de Lafayette's visit to the school in 1824 (included in this reprint edition).[7] He also loved to draw, as we see here in his extraordinary depiction of Benjamin Franklin. With Smith's multiple talents and broad curiosity, his teachers must have labored to provide him with constant and escalating challenges.

As he culminated his fortunate years at the Free School, Smith set his sights on a medical and scientific education. Rejected, however, by the medical schools at Columbia College and Geneva, New York because of his race, he embarked for the more welcoming University of Glasgow, Scotland in 1832 at the age of nineteen. During his five years in Glasgow, Smith thrived as what we today would call an "international student" abroad, learning not only from books and libraries, but from life. By the mid-1830s the abolition movement had taken firm hold in England, Scotland, and Ireland, and Smith joined the Glasgow Emancipation Society as a charter member and active force. In rapid succession, the young American earned degrees of B. A. (1835), M. A. (1836), and M. D. (1837).[8] From this conquest of scholarly and racial obstacles, Smith returned home to New York a remarkably well-educated, ambitious, confident twenty-four-year old intellectual. He was also more than ready, he thought, to do battle with American racism.

Smith set himself up as the first university-trained black physician in the United States. He opened a successful interracial practice and pharmacy on West Broadway, married Malvina Barnet, the daughter of a prominent black family that shared his educational strivings, and quickly settled into a relatively comfortable middle-class life. Numerous meetings were held in his honor to pay tribute to the young scholar and doctor. One such meeting in upstate Troy, New York celebrated how Smith's achievement demanded the "respect and admiration of the enlightened world." Even if he had so desired, Smith could now no longer avoid the dual roles now of learned doctor and black activist. A New York City gathering in his honor reminded him that he must perform as both an "ornament to your country" and an "advocate for the oppressed."[9] Facing the many restraints of racism—and though he generally shunned the public limelight—Smith strove for the rest of his career to personify the intellectual capacity of his race at the same time that he so dearly wanted recognition of his universal, human achievements.

Those achievements, though still not well-known today, were many. In his daily life, Smith served Manhattan residents as a druggist and general physician. But his career as an abolitionist and a writer left a more visible mark. The breadth of his activities included participation in organizations devoted to black self-help and to social and moral reform of urban life. He also devoted himself to literary societies, antislavery politics, the Negro Convention movement, and especially the elevation of free black children through education. As early as 1838, Smith was a main speaker at the American Antislavery Society's annual convention. By the mid-1840s, he was treasurer of the Society for the Promotion of Education Among Colored Children, the founder of the Statistics Institute, a leading light in the Philomathean Literary Society, the staff physician for the New York Colored Orphan Asylum, and a chief administrator of the abolitionist Gerrit Smith's ill-fated scheme to relocate several thousand blacks to a huge donation of land in upstate New York. He even found time to compete in serious chess tournaments.[10]

It was by dint of his pen, however, and through the force of ideas, that Smith endures as a historical figure. His essays included scientific treatises on phrenology (the so-called "racial science" of measuring skulls, physical characteristics and distinctions between races); the effects of climate and geography on human longevity; and a bold critique of Thomas Jefferson's racial ideas in the founder's *Notes on the State of Virginia*. A voracious reader of history and of romantic poetry and fiction, he counted Robert Burns, Lord Byron, Washington Irving, and Ralph Waldo Emerson among his favorites, along with Herman Melville. Indeed, in 1856, Smith published a remarkable short critique of Melville's *Moby-Dick* in which he likened the *Pequod*, the novel's whaling ship, to the ship of state in slaveholding America. Both were driven by tragic obsessions, Smith contended, the one a white whale and the other white supremacy, toward a self-propelled destruction.[11]

Smith also published numerous essays on historical and contemporary issues such as Toussaint L'Overture and the Haitian Revolution, the meaning of "citizenship" for blacks in the wake of the Dred Scott decision of 1857, and the impact of European immigration on the economic and social status of blacks in New York City. In 1841, while still only twenty-eight years old, he delivered a brilliant lecture on the Haitian Revolution at the Stuyvesant Institute in Manhattan. Contrary to widespread assumption, Smith argued that the bloodshed and violence of the revolution had not been attributable to the liberation of heretofore restrained black slaves. Slavery itself, he contended, was far "more destructive of human life than the wars, insurrections, and massacres to which it gave birth." Slaveholders in St. Domingue, he wrote, "destroyed no less than 5,000 human beings per annum" by crushing them with labor.[12]

Smith also wrote lengthy introductions to Frederick Douglass's second autobiography, *My Bondage and My Freedom*, and to Garnet's *Memorial Discourse*, offering both former fugitive slaves the kind of intellectual imprimatur they could find nowhere else among black Americans. Finally, perhaps the most revealing of Smith's writings were his semi-regular columns published under the pseudonym "Communipaw" in *Frederick Douglass' Paper* during the 1850s. In a remarkable series of articles entitled "The Heads of the Colored People" (a reference to the absurd theories advanced by phrenology), Smith honored the dignity of common labor among the black masses he witnessed in the New York streets daily. Black laborers represented "not only the bone and sinew," said Smith, "but also the heart and brain of a nation." "A people… whose common destiny is labor," he contended, "is of necessity destined to advance civilization." In individual vignettes, Smith celebrated ship stewards, washerwomen, boot polishers, whitewashers, and even a "legless newspaper vendor," among many others. He exalted these common folk for their work ethic, their dignity, their skill, and their role in boosting racial pride by "battling against slavery and caste."[13] At the end of his sketches, Smith's humble workers would often kneel in prayer or march off to church in Sunday finery. No African American had ever written such compelling stories about the value of labor and the heroism of ordinary human striving.

No issue animated Smith as a writer-reformer quite as much as education. He constantly stressed a program of self-improvement and community uplift among northern free blacks. Just as the African Free School No. 2 had been so pivotal in his own early life, Smith placed his hopes in schools for black youth. In 1848, he wrote that he would "fling whatever energy I have into the cause of colored children, that they may be better and more thoroughly taught than their parents were." Equal to owning land or the right to vote, schools and education, he argued, were the only true "caste abolisher," the only secure path to black self-reliance and equality. Smith feared the ravages of "brutal ignorance" among black urban youth of the 1840s and 1850s, averring that the denial of an education was an "atrocity that would forever disfigure their fame." Smith wanted education to be the passion of the age as much as abolitionism itself. "So deeply" did he and his former Free School classmates "feel the want of education in themselves," he insisted, "that they would run all risks, make any sacrifice to secure it."[14] Whatever subject he took up, Smith's writing style exhibited a poignant wit, a tendency toward satire, a controlled outrage against racism of all kinds, a strong sense of moral responsibility, and a deep faith in education and human reason. Although his faith was sorely tested, he really believed that the light of human knowledge could conquer the darkness of human nature.

As an active participant in antislavery politics in the late 1850s, and in some despair in the wake of the Supreme Court's declaration in *Dred Scott* (1857) that blacks had neither rights nor a future as citizens in America, Smith welcomed the Civil War when it came in 1861. By 1863 he fell ill and during much of 1864-65 was confined to his home in New York. He died before his time of heart disease on November 17, 1865 at the age of fifty-two.

Death denied Smith the fulfillment of one of his dreams, for he had once written that "no life would so entirely agree with my tastes and desires… as a quiet professorship in an advancing institution of learning." In 1859, after considerable negotiation, Smith turned down a professorship at Central College in McGrawville, New York because the new black school could barely afford to pay a salary. But in 1863, Bishop of the African Methodist Episcopal Church Daniel A. Payne offered Smith the position of his choosing at Wilberforce College in Ohio. Smith gladly consented to leave his medical practice in New York, possibly in the wake of the draft riots, and selected the chair in, of all disciplines, anthropology. Wilberforce reserved the "first cottage" for Smith for more than a year, though he never arrived to pursue his dreams of teaching.[15]

Smith was all but forgotten in the national historical record, but not by his African American contemporaries. When Frederick Douglass recorded the names of those who had most influenced his life, he unhesitatingly declared: "foremost, I place the name of James McCune Smith." Before Smith, admitted Douglass, blacks had not known a "thoroughly educated man amongst us." Above all, the doctor and essayist, Douglass wrote, had "demonstrated the possibility of education for colored men."

Like Douglass, Alexander Crummell, accomplished theologian and Smith's former classmate at the Free School, later labeled Smith the "most learned Negro of his day."[16] This was a particularly telling tribute, for it came from the single man who might have competed for such a distinction.

In this presentation book of the African Free School we are offered a rare glimpse into the connections between childhood intellectual endeavors and the adult, mature creativity and expression of a late Enlightenment thinker such as James McCune Smith. At the same time, we can see a stunning example of the native-born, original genius that Ralph Waldo Emerson yearned for in his 1837 essay, "The American Scholar." America, like the old world, must cultivate its own intellect, its own history, its own truth out of its own landscape and experience, Emerson contended, so that it too might produce a new "Man Thinking" who would not be, as Europe expected, "timid, imitative, tame." America's Man Thinking, like all others, would embody three great sources of knowledge: he would be a deep observer of "nature," he would closely read history and draw endlessly on the past from "books," and he would make life itself, his own "action," the scholar's ultimate vocation.[17]

From Emerson's trinity of raw materials—nature, books, and action, the very stuff from which he posited that scholars are formed—we can see McCune Smith emerge as the scientist, the literary historian, and the activist. And Emerson, who so desired to see such scholars in America, might easily have been describing the New York physician and fellow essayist as he concluded his work entitled "The American Scholar: "We will walk on our own feet; we will work with our own hands; we will speak our own minds. The study of letters shall be no longer a name for pity, for doubt, and for sensual indulgence.... A nation of men will for the first time exist, because each believes himself inspired by the Divine Soul which also inspires all men."[18] Smith read Emerson. Then he courageously lived out the call to be the American Scholar.

DAVID W. BLIGHT
Yale University

JAMES O. HORTON
George Washington University

[1] Carleton Mabee, *Black Education in New York State from Colonial to Modern Times* (Syracuse, NY: Syracuse University Press, 1979), 1-13.

[2] Ellis O. Knox, "The Origin and Development of the Negro Separate School," *The Journal of Negro Education* 16, no.3 (Summer 1947): 269-79.

[3] Ivan D. Steen, "Education to What End? An Englishman Comments on the Plight of Blacks in the 'Free' States, 1830," *Afro-Americans in New York Life and History* 7, no. 1 (January 1983): 55-60; Introduction to excerpt from Thomas Hamilton, *Men and Manners in America* (Edinburgh: W. Blackwood, 1833), I:91-98; Roi Ottley & William J. Weatherby, *The Negro in New York* (New York: Praeger, 1967), 63-64.

[4] James McCune Smith, *A Memorial Discourse by Henry Highland Garnet*, (Philadelphia: Joseph M. Wilson, 1865), 21-23. Thomas Hamilton, *Men and Manners in America* (Edinburgh: W. Blackwood, 1833), I:90-91.

[5] Alexander Crummell, *The Eulogy on Henry Highland Garnet* (New York: 1882), 25. This story provides a context for Garnet's later militancy.

[6] Jonston R. McKay, "James McCune Smith of New York," *The College Courant: The Journal of the Glasgow University Graduate Association* 23, no. 47 (1971): 26-27; Garnet, *Memorial Discourse*, 24-26.

[7] The Toussaint speech is reprinted in Charles C. Andrews, *The History of the New York African Free School* (1830; repr. New York: Arno Press, 1969), 52.

[8] McKay, "James McCune Smith," 26; David W. Blight, "In Search of Learning, Liberty, and Self-Definition: James McCune Smith and the Ordeal of the Antebellum Black Intellectual," *Afro-Americans in New York Life and History* 9, no. 2 (July 1985): 8-9.

[9] *Colored American*, October 14, 28, 1837. See John Stauffer, *The Black Hearts of Men: Radical Abolitionists and the Transformation of Race* (Cambridge: Harvard University Press, 2002), 125.

[10] See Blight, "In Search of Learning, Liberty, and Self-Definition," 9.

[11] See James McCune Smith, "The Influence of Climate Upon Longevity," *Hunt's Merchants Magazine,* (April-May, 1846), intended as a direct reply to tee assertions of black inferiority by John C. Calhoun; Smith, "On the Fourth Query of Thomas Jefferson's Notes on Virginia," *Anglo-African Magazine* 1, no. 8 (August 1859), 225-38; Smith, "Civilization: Its Dependence on Physical Circumstances," *Anglo-African Magazine* 1, no. 1 (January 1859): 5-17. For the critique of *Moby-Dick*, see *Frederick Douglass' Paper* (hereafter cited as *FDP*), March 7, 1856. Also see a series of letters in *Liberator*, February, 16, 23, 1844, and *New-York Tribune*, January 11, 19, 1844, originally delivered as a lecture series, "Freedom and Slavery for Africans." These letters are reprinted in full in Carter G. Woodson, ed., *The Mind of the Negro as Reflected in Letters Written During the Crisis, 1800-1860* (Washington, DC, 1926), 270-80. On Smith as writer, also see Stauffer, *Black Hearts of Men*, 65-70.

[12] Smith, *A Lecture on the Haytien Revolutions: With a Sketch of the Character of Toussaint L'Overture* (New York: Daniel Fanshaw, 1841), 17-20, 23; Smith, "Citizenship," *Anglo-African Magazine* 1, no. 5 (May 1859): 144-50; Smith, "The German Invasion," *Anglo-African Magazine* 1, no. 2 (February 1859), 44-52. See Stauffer, *Black Hearts of Men*, 126.

[13] Smith, "Civilization," 8; *FDP*, March 25, June 17, September 30, December 24, 1852. See Blight, "In Search of Learning, Liberty, and Self-Definition," 11-12.

[14] Smith to Gerrit Smith, May 12, 1848, Gerrit Smith Papers, University of Syracuse Library; *Douglass Monthly*, March, 1859; Smith's introduction, Garnet, *Memorial Discourse,* 27.

[15] Smith to Gerrit Smith, January 13, 1864, January 29, 1859, March 9, 1859, Gerrit Smith Papers; Daniel Alexander Payne, *Recollections of Seventy Years*, (1888; repr. New York: Arno Press, 1968), 82-84. See Blight, "In Search of Learning, Liberty, and Self-Definition," 18-19.

[16] Frederick Douglass, *Life and Times of Frederick Douglass*, (1882; repr. New York: Collier, 1962), 468; Crummell, *Eulogy on Henry Highland Garnet*, 6.

[17] Ralph Waldo Emerson, "The American Scholar," in Larzer Ziff, ed., *Ralph Waldo Emerson: Selected Essays* (New York: Penguin, 1982), 85-100, 104.

[18] Ibid., 104-05.

Performing Freedom at the New York African Free School

"In all cases," James McCune Smith wrote in 1865, "the school-house, and school-boy days, settle the permanent characteristics, establish the level, gauge the relative, mental and moral power of the man in after life; especially it was so in this school."[1] McCune Smith, a vital force in the antebellum black community, and the first African American to receive a medical degree, was speaking of his alma mater, the New York African Free School. It was an extraordinary institution that sought to prepare black children for the free status that New York State law promised to all slaves by 1827; training in leadership proved a vital segment of that preparation.

Judging by the accomplishments of many of the school's graduates, who went on to become leading figures in medicine, religion and the arts, the mission was a resounding success. The records of the school represent the juvenilia of an emerging black elite, many of whom, like missionary Alexander Crummell, radical abolitionist Henry Highland Garnet, physician James McCune Smith, actor Ira Aldridge, and artist Patrick Reason, achieved a level of accomplishment previously unknown to African Americans.

The graduates of the African Free School—boys and girls of about fourteen years of age—faced an uncertain array of possibilities in antebellum New York. Immigrants were coming to the city at a brisk pace, and competition for work was fierce. Gaining higher education was a difficult task for African Americans in the early nineteenth century, and many of those who did gain advanced degrees had to overcome numerous obstacles, ranging from passive but potent antagonism, to violent attacks. The difficulties the students faced, then, render their later successes still more remarkable. Looking back, we find that the school-day experiences of these students were of great significance. It is during these years, after all, that a generation of young black people found the means to create lives of great moral purpose and substantial historic weight.

Fortunately, the New-York Historical Society has preserved a rich archive of materials pertaining to the African Free School—materials that allow us to catch a glimpse of the complex negotiations between students, teachers, and the larger New York community as they worked to define what freedom would look like for black New Yorkers. The facsimiles in this volume represent a precise reproduction of volume 4 of the AFS records—a bound collection of the students' own work likely presented to the public on "Examination Days." This essay draws from the history of the school, and the materials found in both volume 4 and volume 3 (found only in the New-York Historical Society library collection) to offer some possible strategies and frameworks for interpreting the beautiful images, essays, and poetry uncovered in volume 4, and presented here as *"Hope is the First Great Blessing": Leaves from the New York African Free School*.

Examination Days were a yearly gathering that anticipated the modern practice of school plays put on for parents. On these occasions, the New York African Free School treated benefactors, parents, and the local press to a series of performances and presentations designed to showcase the students' blooming abilities. It was in this semi-public arena that the students, their work, and the efforts of their instructors, were put on display for the approval of those footing the bill. While a successful day would display conventional intellect, and elicit sympathy, the students on stage would also be testing boundaries: could they actively debunk racial stereotypes? Would whites be uncomfortable if the students appeared somehow "too" advanced?

The records found at the New-York Historical Society are particularly important because they provide insight into the people who truly made the school a success—the students. While the white trustees of the New-York Manumission Society were undoubtedly an essential and important component during the New York African Free School's successful tenure, it is important to remember that African Americans were the ones truly responsible for making the school such a success. The New-York Manumission Society provided the tools and resources that were essential in order for these students to receive an education, but it was the students' own intelligence, perseverance and ingenuity that allowed them to build upon that foundation and emerge as local, national, and international leaders. Faced with crushing workloads, and the threat of punishment and loss of income, black New Yorkers nevertheless made education a top priority throughout the nineteenth century. As James McCune Smith wrote, "[s]o deeply did they [African Americans] feel the want of education in themselves, that they would run all risks, make any sacrifice, to secure it."[2]

As readers of this volume, we occupy a position similar to the one held by Examination Day audiences almost two hundred years ago. We are provided with exemplary pieces of student work that we scrutinize in order to glean some deeper meaning about the students themselves. We, however, have the additional benefit of historical hindsight—we know that these playful skits, lovely drawings, and methodical displays of mathematical prowess provide a means of understanding a generation that would move from subservience to leadership during one of the most trying periods in our nation's history.

Even with the benefit of hindsight, interpreting the NYAFS records is a difficult task. When looking at the beautiful sketches of pastoral hunters, exciting renditions of warships, and respectful portraits of Benjamin Franklin found in Volume 4: *Hope is the First Blessing*, our first impulse might be to see these images as the extemporaneous expressions of young children recording what interested only themselves. However, the process of drawing instruction in the early nineteenth century emphasized skill in copying over originality. The vast majority of the images found in this volume was copied out of a drawing instruction manual: simply put, we have a portrait of Benjamin Franklin before us today because the drawing instructor felt that Benjamin Franklin was a suitable subject for that day.

Yet, in spite of these limitations, these images offer us insight into the experience of these young students in two ways. First, we can glean the priorities and values of the instructors by considering the choices that they made. For instance, we have no portrait of Toussaint L'Ouverture, the black leader of the Haitian Revolution, and, who, like Benjamin Franklin, was a major player on the world stage in the late eighteenth century. Perhaps it was difficult to find a suitable portrait of L'Ouverture, or perhaps the instructor felt that a black revolutionary wasn't a good role model for young black students preparing for their freedom in a slave nation. Indeed, nowhere in the records do we find a portrait of any black subject.

We must also remember that even if they had little control over the subject matter of their lessons, the students invariably brought their own experience to the work before them—where, one could posit, the work immediately took on new meanings in their hands. The image on page 43 of the hunter and his dogs, for instance, was a standard scene for European artists enamored with romanticizing country life. However, the image takes on a different tone when we remember students such as Henry Highland Garnet who, with his family, had run away from slavery. For a student like the young Garnet, who went on to become a radical abolitionist, the picture of a white man on a hunt with his dogs could well have conjured up nightmarish associations with the slave-catcher, rather than the idyllic image of pastoral leisure that whites would likely feel the piece conveyed. Similarly, the portrait of Napoleon Francois, Charles Joseph (page 35 in this volume), takes on particular layers of meaning when viewed in light of its execution by New York African Free School students. Caught up in the political turmoil of his father Napoleon Bonaparte's, life, Charles Joseph was exiled to Vienna at the age of four, and encouraged to forget all ties to France. One wonders how young black students, who may well have had their own family histories stolen from them through slavery, might have felt about this young, dispossessed prince, exiled far from his native land.

The written texts (some of which are found in this volume, while others are contained in the unpublished volume 3) present a similar set of questions about author and reception. Because the record-keepers were meticulous about authorship, we can feel fairly confident about discerning between adult-and student-authored texts. What to do with that information is a more difficult question. We can ask ourselves how the white-authored scripts taught students to see themselves, their heritage, and their future, but we can only guess at how the students themselves might have felt about these lessons. When we are presented with the students' own words in original essays and poetry, we are left to wonder at the extent to which they felt free to express themselves. In the end, both the scripted and the original pieces provide insight into what the students might have thought about the extraordinary role they were playing. They also shed light upon the sort of roles the audience may have wanted them to play.

The students were working in the midst of a rapidly evolving city, and within an environment that was decidedly ambivalent about the prospect of a substantial and participatory population of black New Yorkers. The city had passed a gradual manumission law in 1799, but slavery was still legal in certain circumstances until 1827. Funded by the New-York Manumission Society, whose members included some of the wealthiest and best educated white men in the city, an explicit part of the Manumission Society's mission after 1809 included the allocation of funds to the New York African Free School toward the employment of white instructors, who would teach poor black children how best to achieve the privileges and respectability of the predominantly white middle class.

Yet there remained considerable tension between the social reality students faced as members of a persecuted minority, and their future aspirations as members of a well-educated, prosperous and respectable middle class. In Volume Three of the AFS records, the valedictory address of Margaret Addle (written for her by her schoolmaster, C.C. Andrews) reveals such tension. Her speech shifts between pride in her accomplishments and anxiety over her family's continued vulnerability as black people in a slave nation. Beginning with her display of elocutionary talent, Margaret asked the audience to view her and her myriad of skills as evidence of the potential embodied in black people throughout the nation.

I appear before you, as regards myself under very interesting circumstances. It is to take my leave of my School Mates and much endeared teachers. In doing this, I feel it difficult to suppress those feelings which such an occasion is calculated to produce on a heart sensible of obligations so numerous as those which I am under to the gentlemen who support, and the teachers who have had the immediate superintendence of, the institution.

The advantages which this school is calculated to afford to the children of color, have on former occasions been presented to your view. I therefore shall be excused from repeating them. I need only to point you to those specimens, and remind you of the exercises this day exhibited before you, to demonstrate a truth which must at no distant period find its way to the hearts of the most incredulous viz. That the African race, though by too many of their fellow men have long been, [and] still are, held in a state, the most degrading to humanity, and nevertheless, endowed by the same almighty power that made us all, with intellectual capacities, not inferior to any of the grater human family.[3]

From what we can surmise, Margaret's demeanor likely altered as her words shift from the proud valedictory address of a schoolgirl, to the panicked pleadings of a child for whom the auction block poses an unbearable threat.

In looking round on my school mates, I observe one among them who excites my most tender solicitudes.
— It is my Brother.—
John, this I feel to be an occasion which calls up all those tender emotions which he ever has designed should be felt by brother and sister towards each other.
What shall I say to you?
Oh, if I were called to part with you as some poor girls have, to part with their equally dear kindred, and each of us (like them) to be forcibly conveyed away into wretched slavery never to see each other again—-but I must forbear—Thank heaven it is not, no is not the case with us; nor have I ever the anxiety which the circumstances of leaving you under the charge of strangers would produce. No, I leave you to receive instruction, advice reproof, and every other salutary means of informing your mind and correcting your morals, from well known, and long tried friends; be obedient, diligent and studious and, when the period shall arrive for you to take your leave of this school. I trust it will be under circumstances no less affecting to you, than the present is to me.

Reading this scripted performance now, one might grow frustrated at the manner in which such a speech, penned by adults, undermines Margaret's innate abilities by raising the specter of slavery, a tactic that reduces the speaker from accomplished graduate to helpless child. Yet when we consider the context in which the speech was given, the juxtaposition of slave and student might not be so contradictory. Although slavery was on the wane in New York, the fears Margaret describes were very real for many black New Yorkers. Kidnapping of free blacks by unscrupulous traders was a grave and persistent danger. Much of the work of the school's founding institution, the New-York Manumission Society, dealt with precisely this threat. Indeed, numerous cases called upon the Manumission Society's prestigious membership, and all their legal and financial clout, to prosecute kidnappers and aid kidnapping victims.

Other performances were lighter in tone, however, eschewing the terror of slavery for the fun of childish display. Elsewhere in Volume Three of the AFS records, for instance, we find a particularly playful dialogue performed by twin girls in 1821. The piece, like Margaret's, was written for the girls by Charles C. Andrews, their schoolmaster. One can imagine the two girls, dressed in their Sunday best, speaking in unison to a charmed audience:

Ladies and Gentlemen here you see
As pretty a sight as well can be.
We look alike eyes nose and chins
No wonder this for we are twins.
We live as sisters ought to do
We feel as though we are two
We seldom grieve our parents' heart
And seldom from each other part

'Tis said of twins, in days of old,
From thirst of fame or love of gold
They formed two bands resolv'd to see
Which should obtain the victory,
So furious grew the wicked strife,
That Remus yielded up his life.
Rome's famous name to the other owes,
For he was named Romulus
Both Romulus and his Slain brother
Were wicked children of one mother
(One concludes as follows)
O never let us, sister dear,
By disaffection cause a tear
Tho' Father's poor and Mother too,
And live by work they find to do,
They work and strive to earn our bread,
And find us, house, and clothes, and bed
May we repay them with our love,
And duteous children always prove

(To the Company)
Dear friends in sable skins you find
Two children who possess one mind
So formed by nature to agree
That none more happy are than we.[4]

When taken on an elementary level, the performance (replete with stage directions) constitutes a lighthearted diversion for an audience who were likely amused by the girls' identical appearances and recitation. Yet the poem also contains some provocative elements. Members of the audience who sat back and watched two young, poor, black girls compare themselves to the mythological founder of ancient Rome were also witnessing a remarkably savvy play for equality. Their carefree appearance and humorous presentation might well have prompted the audience to nod and laugh in response to the very words through which the girls tacitly laid claim to the literary legacy of classical mythology—a legacy long prized as evidence of white superiority.

At other moments, the students do speak in their own voice, as in the playful and pointed poem written by Andrew R. Smith, and found on page 17 of the facsimile text that follows this essay.

Smith, a 14-year-old valedictorian, creates a poem that moves from the moral admonitions he had likely learned at school, to a mischievous nonchalance about how outsiders might view his work.

On the Fair

The work of children here you find,
The fruit of labour, and of mind;
The month is pat, the day is come,
And he that gaines [sic] shall have the sum

Although our minds are weak and feeble,
Some can use a knife or needle;
If fortune by my side will stand,
I mean to join the happy band

A girl can make a frock or coat,
A boy a pretty little boat;
Another girl a pretty quilt,
A handsome cap, or gown of silk.

To excel we all will work and strive,
Till to perfection we arrive;
Many will work and strive in vain,
The fifty tickets to obtain

Our little fair to us is great,
As any other in the state;
It is a cheerful time to some,
Though idle scholars will not come.

The child that comes to this good school
Should never rest an idle fool;
Though there were many once were so,
We find them daily wiser grow.

The beauties of our little fair,
You will not know if your'e [sic] not there
It will be taking too much time
To enter all the things in rhyme,

P.S. You'll find mistakes I do not doubt,
And if you do please leave them out.

Although we obviously cannot recapture the moment of performance, it seems likely that Smith's final couplet drew laughter from the audience—and from his fellow students. Considering the pressure these students felt to impress their benefactors, and to further the cause of racial equality, Smith's wry request that his auditors ignore his mistakes emerges as a remarkable display of confidence, and even of courage. In a coda to this poem, Smith explains that the piece won him the considerable reward of 50 tickets. Such tickets, in addition to their value as a token of excellence, could be cashed in for any number of little trinkets, such as an ink stand or pinbox. Risky as they may have been, Smith's cheeky sentiments about the school won him the approbation of his teachers.

James Field's 1819 valedictory address is far less cheerful, however. According to the copy found in Volume Three of the school records, this speech was spoken by Field, but written by Rueben Leggett, a white man. Field begins, much like Margaret, with a traditional gesture of gratitude and pride in his status as class valedictorian. "Permit me," he writes, "my very respectable auditors, in this opening upon your attention to remark, that I am happy in having been one of the favoured number who have enjoyed the blessed advantages of the institution." His tone then changes, and like Margaret, he asks for the audience's sympathy. In this instance however, it is not the imagined peril of slavery that poses the problem, but rather the everyday experience of prejudice and attendant poverty that faced young black graduates who had difficulty finding work:

> But I crave your sympathy for myself and for my School mates, for I feel that we need it.
> Had I the mind of a Lock[e] and the eloquence of a Chatham
> Still would there not be in the minds of some an immense distance that would divide me from one of a White Skin—
> What signifies it? Why should I strive hard, and acquire all the constituents of man, If the prevailing genius of the land admits as such, but in an inferior degree, —Pardon me if I feel insignificant and weak—Pardon me if I feel discouragement to oppress me to the very earth. Am I arrived at the end of my education? Just upon the event of setting out in the world? Of commencing some honest pursuit by which to earn a comfortable subsistence?
> What are my prospects? And to what turn my hand?
> Will I be a mechanic? No one will employ me, White boys won't work with me—will I be a merchant? No one will have me in his office—white clerks won't associate with me—Drudgery and servitude then are my prospects—can you be surprised at my discouragement?[5]

While it is tempting to read the above excerpts as proof of the way the schoolchildren really felt, like so many historical documents, these pieces don't allow for such an unequivocal reading. James Field's lament was written for him by Rueben Leggett, a white man who likely had motives of his own. Perhaps the scriptwriter may have viewed the valedictory address as a fruitful moment to move audience members to offer graduates a job. Perhaps the scriptwriter was one of a growing number of the Manumission Society membership amenable to the idea of sending free black people back to Africa, rather than requiring them to face the hardships born of racial prejudice in the U.S. There is also the possibility that this script was written as a means of placating the school's funders and excusing the poor placement rate of some of the school's graduates. Finally, this script could have been the product of sympathetic conversations between white administrators and black students, many of whom were almost certainly encountering difficulty finding work in a city rife with racial prejudice.

In some respects, then, the scripted performances of these children might seem hopelessly conflicted. Yet it is true that all schoolwork, not just that of these ambitious and courageous students, is mediated by the directions of the instructor and the desires of the community. Children, after all, learn by imitating and absorbing the wishes and agendas of those around them. And yet, within and among those competing and contradictory demands, there are glimmers of an emerging sense of identity and autonomy. Turning to page sixteen in the facsimile text provided in this book, one comes across a passage written, and likely performed, for an audience, by thirteen-year old William Seaman. In it, the young boy seems to take particular pleasure from detailing the unrivalled power of the African Lion:

On the Lion

The Lion is a noble creature,
And has a strong terrifick feature;
This roaring which is loud as thunder,
Strikes all around with fear and wonder.

On Afric's dark and sultry shore,
This mighty beast is heard to roar,
And oft on dry and barren grounds,
He most majestically stands.

He prowls and roams about at night,
And travelers tremble, all with fright;
They dare not turn about to fly,
Thinking that he is very nigh.

He roams the desert far and wide,
His faithful dam close by his side;
The strongest beast they will attack
And with their paw will break their back.

As the creation of one of the school's best students, this passage offers a possible glimpse into one child's attempt to find a place for himself, a place that would acknowledge his African ancestry, the legacy of slavery, and the desire to showcase African American potential. In a society where blacks were testing the boundaries of freedom, but still lived in fear of kidnapping or assault by whites, the lion provides an image of unfettered African power. In Seaman's words, it is the absolute master of his environment: all encroachers should "tremble, all with fright," if they are audacious enough to trespass upon his territory. Interestingly, the lion here is not a solitary hunter, a figure that seems likely to appeal to a young boy. Instead, the mighty lion is joined in the last stanza by his "faithful dam." The concluding lines depict a pair of equals, male and female, whose separate strengths combine to make a formidable team. Together, they possess the ability to attack "the strongest beast." With a unifying gesture, male and female bodies strike as one, as with "their paw" they break the back of their hapless opponent.

There are many stories still to uncover about the New York African Free School, but many of the ones that we have found so far, and that are included within the pages of this volume, resonate with young William Seaman's vision of courage, community, and pride.

Anna Mae Duane
University of Connecticut
Thomas Thurston
Yale University

[1] James McCune Smith, "Introduction" Henry Highland Garnet, A Memorial Discourse (Philadelphia: Josepeh M. Wilson, 1865) p 20.

[2] James McCune Smith, "Introduction" p. 27.

[3] I have made silent punctuation corrections where necessary. Records of the New York African Free School. Volume 3, p. 36 & 37.

[4] Records of NYAFS, Volume 3, p 31-32.

[5] NYAFS Records. Vol 3. p 27-29.

LEAVES FROM THE AFRICAN FREE SCHOOL PRESENTATION BOOK
with Annotations by Anna Mae Duane and Thomas Thurston

Henry Hill's

EMBLEM

of

EDUCATION

HENRY   HILL

See in what

Evil plight yon

vine appears;

Nor spreading leaves, nor purple clusters bears,

But if around the elm her arm she throws,

Or by some friendly prop supported grows,

Soon shall the stem be clad with foliage green,

And cluster'd grapes beneath the leaves be seen.

Moral.

Thus prudent care must rear the youthful mind,

By love supported, and with toil refin'd;

'Tis thus alone the human plant can rise;

Unprop'd, it droops, and unsupported, dies.

Performance, No 1.

Nineteenth-century education intertwined the disciplines of penmanship, drawing, and composition. The use of emblems—visual images that inspired moral sentiments—were particularly popular. The tree, for example, symbolizes the possibility—and the fragility—of every student. Only with proper support, or as the poem puts it, "a friendly prop," will a student flourish and bear successful fruit.

To know the "rule of three" in the nineteenth century implied a certain basic competency in mathematics. In his 1859 autobiography, Abraham Lincoln wrote, "Of course when I came of age I did not know much. Still somehow, I could read, write, and cipher to the Rule of Three." The rule of three was a historical form of a proportion. For instance, to apply the rule of three for 3, 9 and 2, one would complete the following problem: 3 is to 9 as 2 is to ___ (6). As the presence of a London merchant in this word problem might suggest, this problem originally appeared in a British arithmetic text book, and was later copied verbatim in a great many American editions.

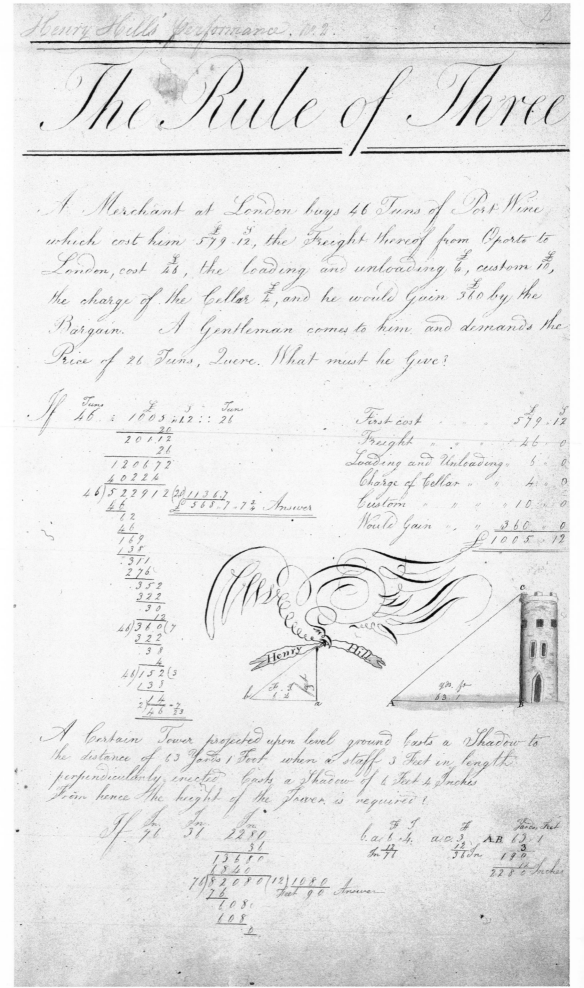

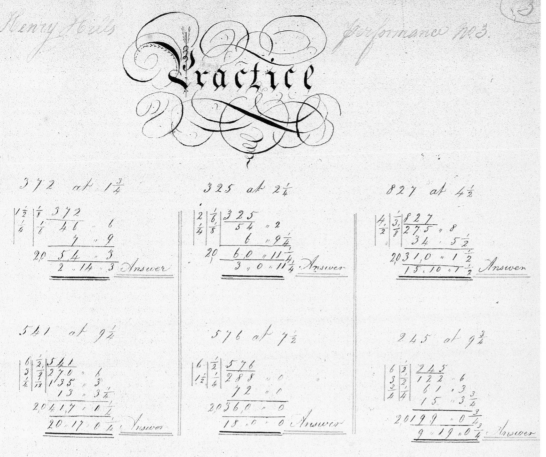

Practice

372 at 1¾   325 at 2⅛   827 at 4½

541 at 9½   576 at 7½   245 at 9¾

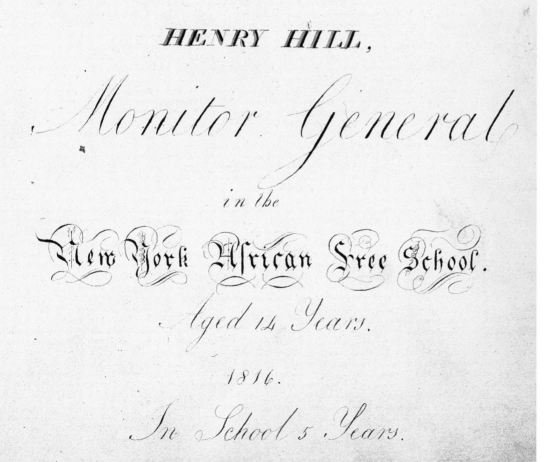

HENRY HILL,

Monitor General

in the

New York African Free School.

Aged 14 Years.

1816.

In School 5 Years.

Henry Hill is here identified as the Monitor General, which means that he would have had a great deal of responsibility over the rest of the class, often performing the same tasks as an adult teacher.

The 1810 US Census records that the Anthony Hill household, an African American family of seven, resided in New York's Third Ward. By 1850, Henry Hill, then 47 years old, was a single man, with no given occupation, living in a multi-racial working class boarding house in New York's 14th Ward. There is no record surviving to indicate whether the education that he received as a young man provided him any form of consolation.

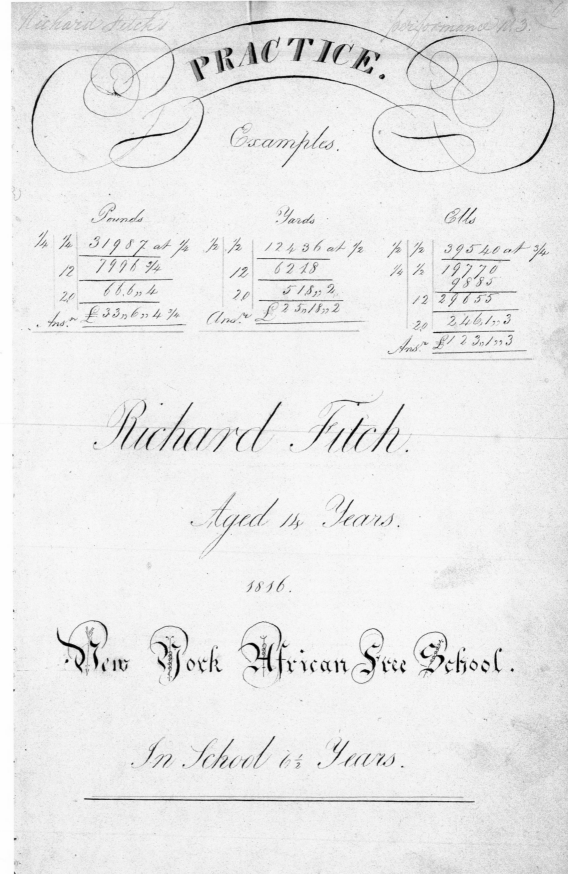

Richard Fitch, a 14-year-old boy, presents math examples matched with lovely penmanship for the 1816 Examination Day. A student at the African Free School for six-and-one-half years, Richard had entered the school the same year as Charles C. Andrews, the school's principal. During those years Richard would have witnessed the excitement that gripped New York City during the War of 1812, when British ships threatened invasion, and he would have been a student when fire destroyed the original school building on Cliff Street. Note that the currency in the examples are marked as British pounds, rather than American dollars.

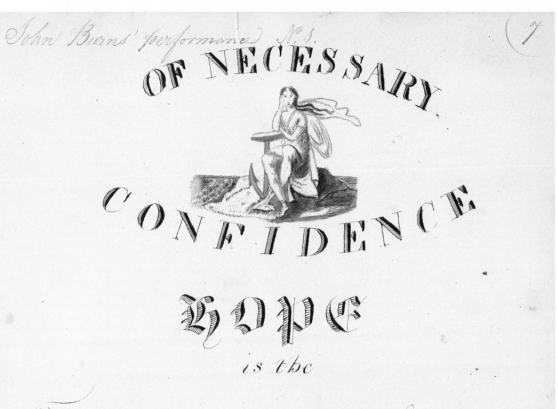

John Burns' performance Nº 4.   7

OF NECESSARY

CONFIDENCE

HOPE

is the

First great blessing

Here below

The only balm to heal corroding woe;

It is the staff of age, the sick man's health;

The prisners freedom, and the poor man's

Wealth

The sailor's safety: lasting as our breath,

It still holds on nor quits us e'en in death.

Moral

Encourage hope, which heals all human care; the last mad folly is a sad despair
If you are wise, that dreadful evil shun, nor fall unpitied, by yourself undone.

As with the document on page one of the presentation book, John Burns's performance, copied from John Huddlestone Wynne's *Choice Emblems,* matches a lovely drawing with an exercise in penmanship and poetry. The poem focuses on the need for hope—a subject that would have likely resonated with many of the students in the school who faced the formidable obstacles of poverty, racial prejudice, and the threat of kidnapping.

This image is likely a rendering of the newly erected school building, built with funds raised by treasurer John Murray after an earlier schoolhouse had burned down in 1814. Charles C. Andrews, the schoolmaster listed on this document, describes how the school's trustees were furnished "with a pressing argument, with which to appeal to the liberality of their fellow-citizens, and to the corporation of the city; and it affords pleasure, to acknowledge with gratitude, that their appeal was not in vain. A grant was obtained on William-Street, on which to build a new school house. . . . This house is sixty feet, by thirty feet wide, and is calculated to accommodate about two hundred scholars. In exactly one year after the abovementioned conflagration, the new schoolhouse was ready for occupation, and in January, 1815, the school, on a comparatively large scale, was resumed with fresh vigour, and increasing interest."

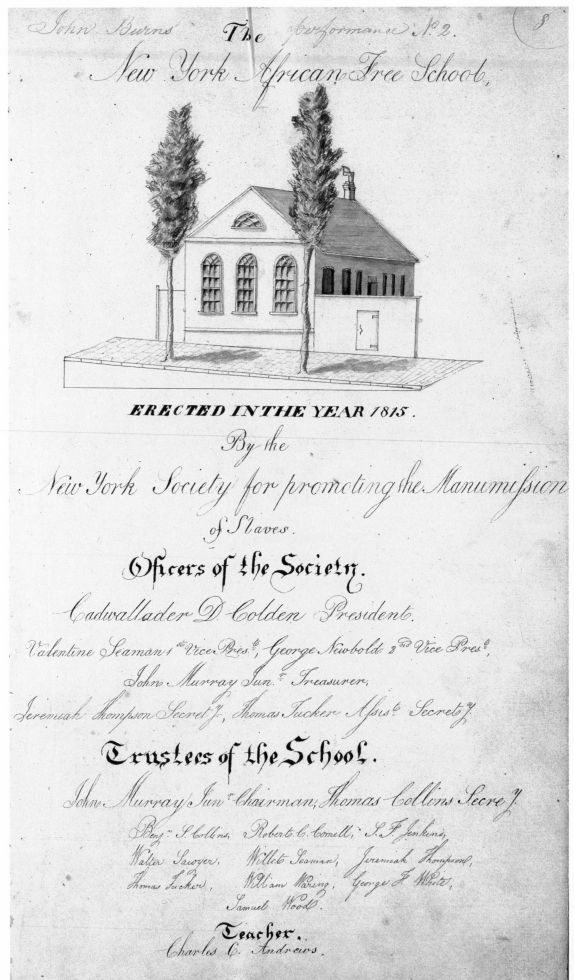

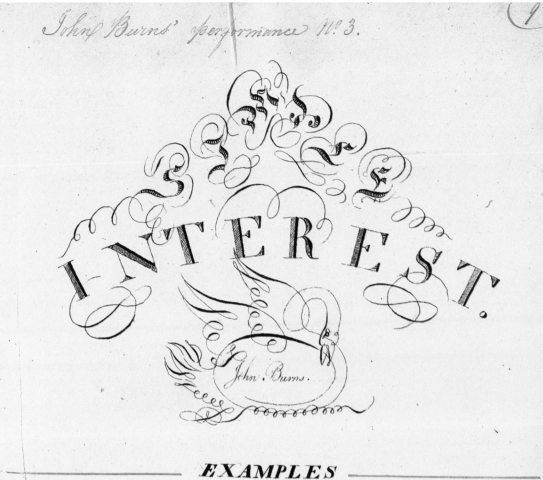

INTEREST.

John. Burns.

John Burns was a talented mathematician, as well as a skillful artist and a careful calligrapher. John's swan flourish was a commonly taught element in penmanship systems of the era. These personalized flourishes demonstrated one's mastery of penmanship and made forged documents easier to detect.

EXAMPLES

What is the Interest of 270 £ 10 S 6 D for one Year, at 5 £ per Cent per Annum?

£ . S . D
270 : 10 : 6
5
13,52 . 12 . 6
20
10.52
12   £ . S . D
6 . 30   13 . 10 . 6 ¼ Answer
4
£ . 2 . 0

What is the Interest of 350 : 17 : 8 for one year, at 6 £ per Cent per Annum?

£ . S . D
350 . 17 . 8
6
21,05 . 6 . 0
20
7 . 0 6
12   £ . S . D
0 . 7 2   21 . 1 . 0 ¼ Answer
4
2 . 8 8

Edward Haines's finely penned copy of "Unhappy Close of Life," by the Scottish poet Robert Blair (1699-1746), was likely taken from *The English Reader: Or Pieces in Prose and Poetry*, a collection of poems and essays widely reprinted throughout the United States during the early 19th Century, and, according to the editor, "designed to assist young persons to read with propriety and effect; to improve their language and sentiments; and to inculcate some of the most important principles of piety and virtue."

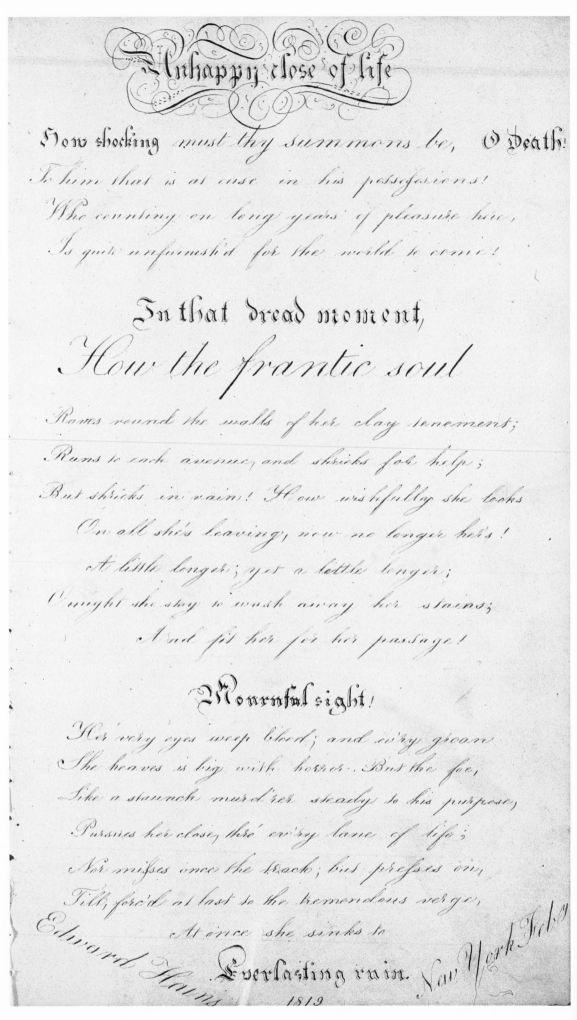

Unhappy close of life

How shocking must thy summons be, O Death!
To him that is at ease in his possessions!
Who counting on long years of pleasure here,
Is quite unfurnish'd for the world to come!

In that dread moment,
How the frantic soul

Raves round the walls of her clay tenement;
Runs to each avenue, and shrieks for help;
But shrieks in vain! How wishfully she looks
On all she's leaving, now no longer her's!
A little longer; yet a little longer;
O might she stay to wash away her stains;
And fit her for her passage!

Mournful sight!

Her very eyes weep blood; and ev'ry groan
She heaves is big with horror. But the foe,
Like a staunch murd'rer steady to his purpose,
Pursues her close, thro' ev'ry lane of life;
Nor misses once the track; but presses on,
Till, forc'd at last to the tremendous verge,
At once she sinks to

Everlasting ruin.

Edward Haines
New York Feb'y
1819

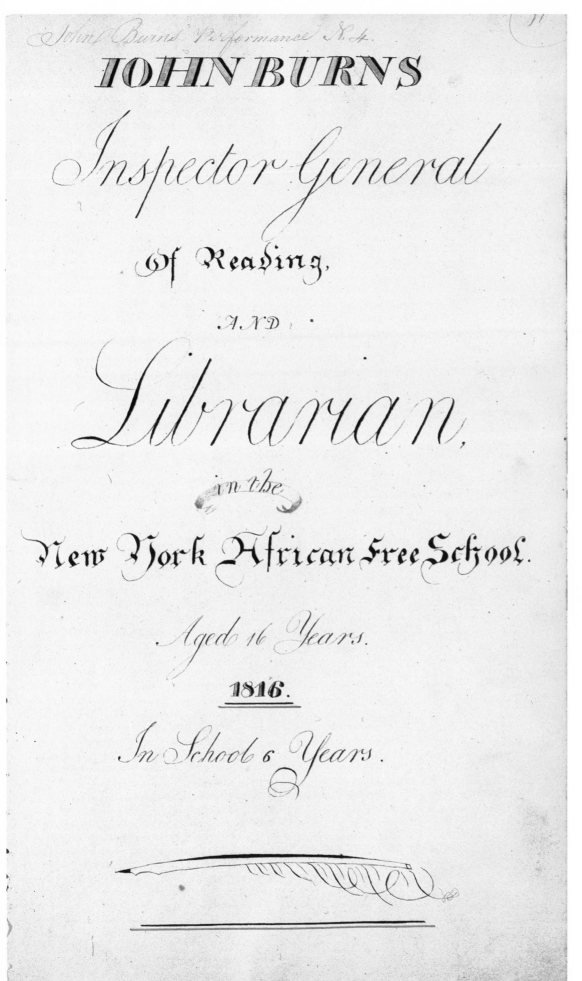

John Burns' Performance No. 4.

IOHN BURNS

Inspector General

Of Reading,

AND

Librarian,

in the

New York African Free School.

Aged 16 Years.

1816.

In School 6 Years.

John Burns was an Inspector General of Reading, which likely meant that he taught lessons and monitored behavior. His age, sixteen years, is a bit older than many of the other star students and vale-dictorians we find in this volume.

In *The History of the New York African Free School*, the school's white principal seems to respond to charges that black students would be unable to assume the level of responsibility that came with being a monitor:

> From long experience it has been found to be no more difficult to select suitable boys for moni-tors among this descrip-tion of children, than among whites; nor is it true that they will not obey the orders and sub-mit to the authority of such monitors, when it is once known that they derive that authority from the master.

As we know from school records, students did per-form their duties admirably. There are several instances where visitors record that, in the absence of the schoolmaster, a teenaged monitor was supervising the entire school with great skill.

In this example of "ciphering to the rule of three," the student uses "federal money" (U.S. Dollars) in the problems, rather than the British currency we find in early examples. Federal money had a complex place in U.S. society during this period. In the eighteenth century, the Continental Congress, along with individual states, had printed great sums of currency in order to fund the Revolutionary War, which left the nation in a state of great inflation and debt. In order to correct this problem, the federal government stopped printing currency, and forbad states from doing so as well. Instead, a intricate—some might say chaotic—system of banks arose. The first bank was created in 1781. By the 1830's, there were over 2,000 banks across the United States, each of which created, and printed, its own currency.

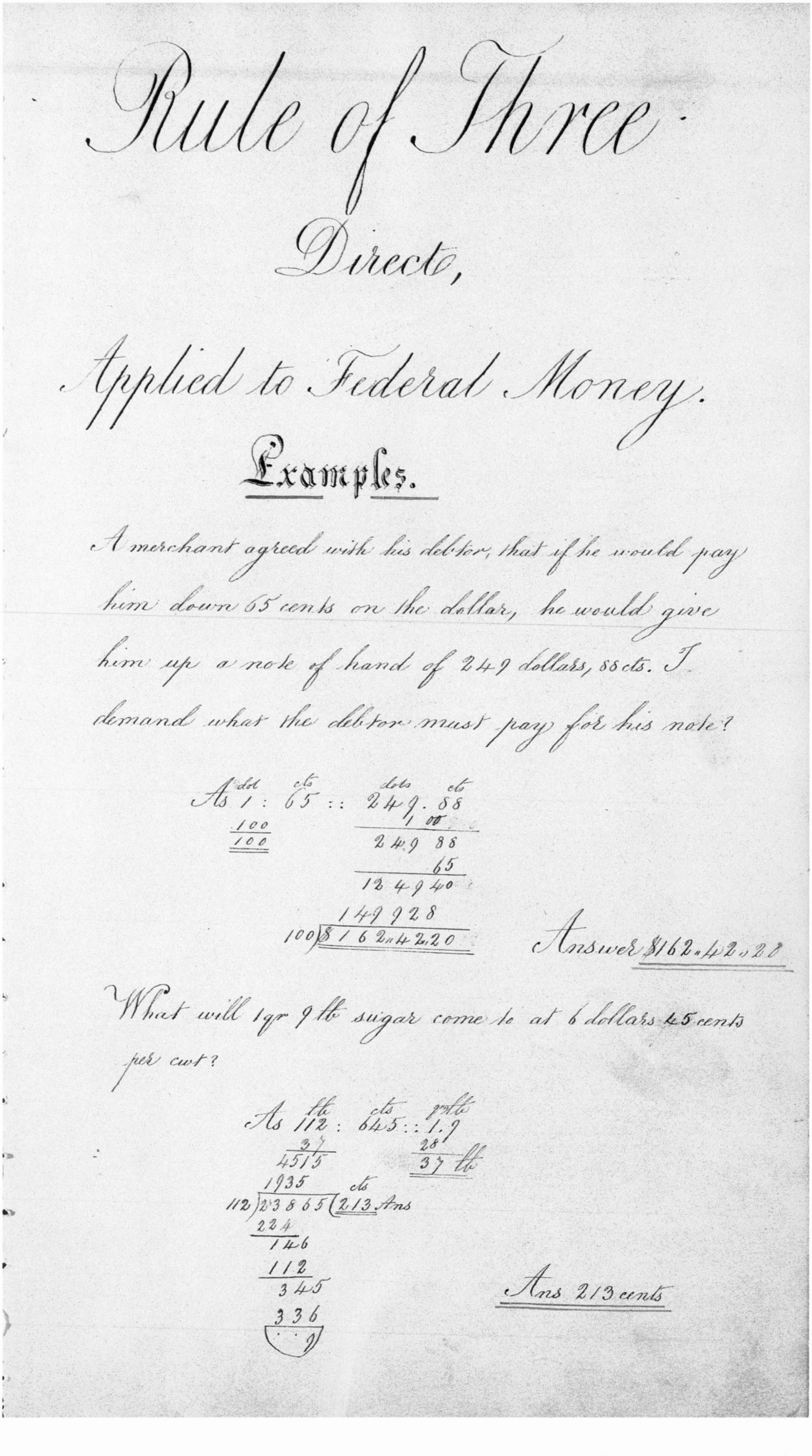

Rule of Three.

Direct,

Applied to Federal Money.

Examples.

A merchant agreed with his debtor, that if he would pay him down 65 cents on the dollar, he would give him up a note of hand of 249 dollars, 88 cts. I demand what the debtor must pay for his note?

$$
\begin{array}{c}
\text{As } 1 : 65 :: 249.88 \\
\end{array}
$$

Answer $162.42.20

What will 1qr 9 lb sugar come to at 6 dollars 45 cents per cwt?

As 112 : 645 :: 1.9

Ans 213 cents

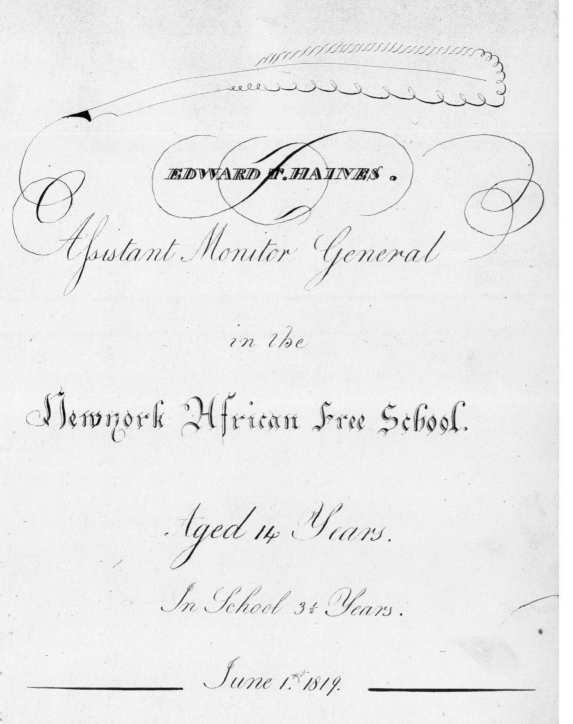

EDWARD T. HAINES.

Assistant Monitor General

in the

New York African Free School.

Aged 14 Years.

In School 3½ Years.

——— June 1st 1819. ———

Edward T. Hains.

Edward T. Haines, clearly a star student, proudly displays his handwriting skill and his title as "Assistant Monitor General," a position that carried significant responsibilities. The 1820 U.S. Census lists an African American "Hains" family with a boy Edward's age living in New York City's Fifth Ward, a west-side neighborhood south of Canal Street that was the home of many free people of color in New York City.

This poem was excerpted from a larger piece by Joseph Addison, "Liberty and Slavery Contrasted." Interestingly, the selection here focuses solely on the happy prospect of liberty, a choice that, in some ways, anticipates the emphasis of many free blacks in the North on local civil rights rather than abolition. The question of whether Northern free blacks should invest their energy in the plight of slaves in the South, rather than in the particular problems of their own communities, continued to be a subject of debate when many of these children grew to adulthood.

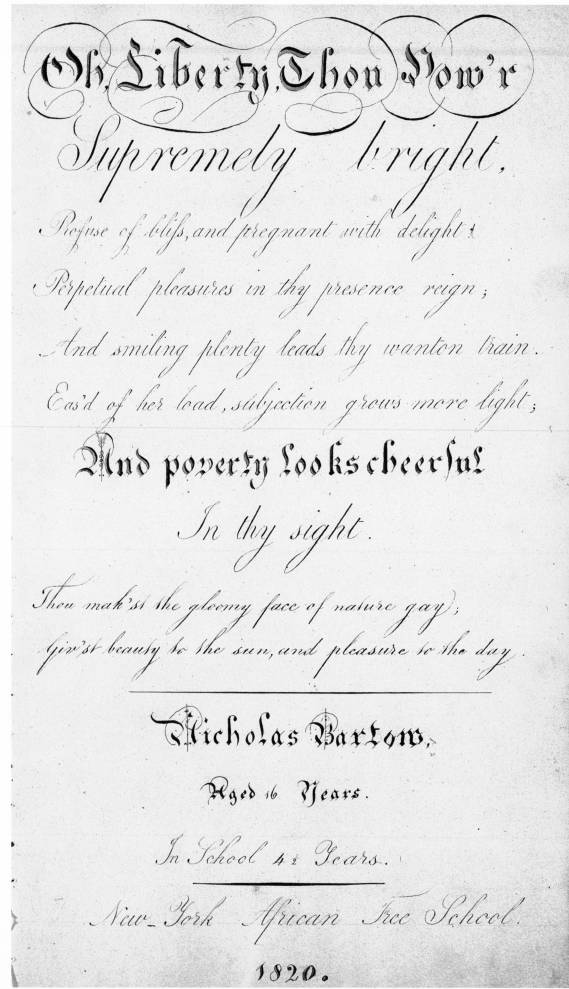

Oh, Liberty, Thou Pow'r

Supremely bright,

Profuse of bliss, and pregnant with delight:

Perpetual pleasures in thy presence reign;

And smiling plenty leads thy wanton train.

Eas'd of her load, subjection grows more light;

And poverty looks cheerful

In thy sight.

Thou mak'st the gloomy face of nature gay;

Giv'st beauty to the sun, and pleasure to the day.

Nicholas Bartow,

Aged 16 Years.

In School 4½ Years.

New-York African Free School.

1820.

FELLOWSHIP.

Fellowship is a rule, by which merchants &c. trading in company with a joint stock, are enabled to ascertain each person's particular share of the gain or loss, in proportion to his share in the joint stock.

By this rule also legacies are adjusted, and the effects of Bankrupts are divided, &c.

Case 1st

When the several stocks in company are considered without regard to time.

Rule.

As the whole sum, or stock
Is to the whole gain or loss,
So is each person's share in stock, &c.
To his share of the gain or loss.

Proof.

The sum of the several shares must equal the gain or loss.

Continued

These math problems deal with potential stock ventures. The prevalence of this sort of example indicates, perhaps, that knowledge of stock trading was considered essential for anyone hoping to enter the middle classes. As many scholars have suggested, capitalism offered a means of freedom, and to a certain extent, equality, for slaves who could work the system in the eighteenth century. By the nineteenth century however, it had become much harder for a slave to buy himself into freedom, or to prosper financially once that freedom was attained.

FELLOWSHIP CONTINUED.

EXAMPLES.

Three merchants, trading together, gained 800 $; As stock was 1200 Dollars, B's 4800 Dollars, and C's 2000 Dollars: what was each man's share of the gain?

A's Stock 1 2 0 0 Dollars,
B's Stock 4 8 0 0 Dollars,
C's Stock 2 0 0 0 Dollars,
Whole Stock 8 0 0 0 Dollars.

$
\begin{array}{ccc}
$ & $ & $ \\
\end{array}
$
A's 8000 : 800 :: 1200
                              800 $
8000)960000(120 A's Share of gain.
        8000
        16000
        16000
              0

A's 8000 : 800 :: 4800
                              800 $
8000)3840000(480 B's Share of gain.
        32000
        64000
        64000
              0

A's 8000 : 800 :: 2000
                              800 $
8000)1600000(200 C's Share of gain.
        16000
              00

PROOF.
A's Share 120
B's Share 480
C's Share 200
$ 800 Answer

A short account of the

LION

This animal is produced in Africa, and the hottest parts of Asia. It is found in the greatest numbers in the scorched and desolate regions of the torrid zone, in the desarts of Zahara and Biledulgerid, and in all the interior parts of the vast continent of Africa. In these desart regions from whence mankind are driven by the rigorous heat of the climate, this animal reigns sole master: Its disposition seems to partake of the ardour of its native soil. Inflamed by the influence of a burning sun, its rage is most tremendous, and its courage undaunted.

The form of the Lion is strikingly bold and majestic: His large and shaggy mane, which he can erect at his pleasure, surrounding his awful front; his huge eye-brows, his round and fiery eye-balls, which, upon the least irritation, seem to glow with peculiar lustre; together with the formidable appearance of his teeth, exhibit a picture of terrefic grandeur which no words can describe.

PAGE 15

"A short Account of the Lion" was likely copied from Caleb Bingham's *The American Preceptor*, a popular school book of the era designed to instruct students in the art of public speaking. Frederick Douglass famously accounts his debt to Caleb Bingham's more famous work, *The Columbian Orator*, which helped to form Douglass's beliefs and persuasive style of public speaking.

See page 23 of the introductory essay by Anna Mae Duane and Thomas Thurston for an in-depth analysis of this poem.

This is an original poem by William Seaman; compare it with the earlier poem on the Lion, taken from a popular schoolbook. This strikingly positive description of an African animal contrasts with the work of pedagogues like the Earl of Chesterfield, otherwise known as Philip Stanhope:

> The Africans are the most ignorant and unpolished people in the world, little better than the lions, tigers and leopards and other wild beasts, which that country produces in great numbers.

Although we cannot tell if William Seaman ever read the work of Philip Stanhope, he was probably familiar with the familiar tactic of conflating Africans with lions. Here he turns that tactic to his advantage, in order to create a noble portrait of African identity.

Original Poetry,

BY

William Seaman Aged 13 Years in the New York African Free School.

On the Lion.

The Lion is a noble creature,
And has a strong terrifick feature;
His roaring which is loud as thunder,
Strikes all around with fear and wonder.

On Afric's dark and sultry shore,
This mighty beast is heard to roar;
And oft on dry and barren sands,
He most majestically stands.

He prowls and roams about at night,
And trav'lers tremble, all with fright;
They dare not turn about to fly,
Thinking that he is very nigh.

He roams the desart far and wide,
His faithful dam close by his side;
The strongest beast they will attack,
And with their paw will break their back.

Original Poetry Continued.
On the Fair.

The work of children here you find,
The fruit of labour, and of mind;
The month is past, the day is come,
And he that gaines shall have the sum.

Although our minds are weak and feeble,
Some can use a knife or needle;
If fortune by my side will stand,
I mean to join the happy band.

A girl can make a frock or coat,
A boy a pretty little boat;
Another girl a pretty quilt,
A handsome cap, or gown of silk.

T'excel we all will work and strive,
Till to perfection we arrive;
Many will work and strive in vain,
The fifty tickets to obtain.

Our little fair to us is great,
As any other in the state;
It is a cheerful time to some,
Though idle scholars will not come.

The child that comes to this good school,
Should never rest an idle fool;
Though there were many once were so,
We find them daily wiser grow.

PAGE 17 & 18

See pages 21–22 of the introductory essay by Anna Mae Duane and Thomas Thurston for analysis of this poem.

Reduction of Vulgar Fractions

Mathematical skill is highlighted by creative presentation and artful penmanship. While a student who indulged in such lovely embellishments when completing math problems today would likely be chastised for "doodling," for the students of the African Free School such flourishes were not only expected, they were worthy of display and admiration.

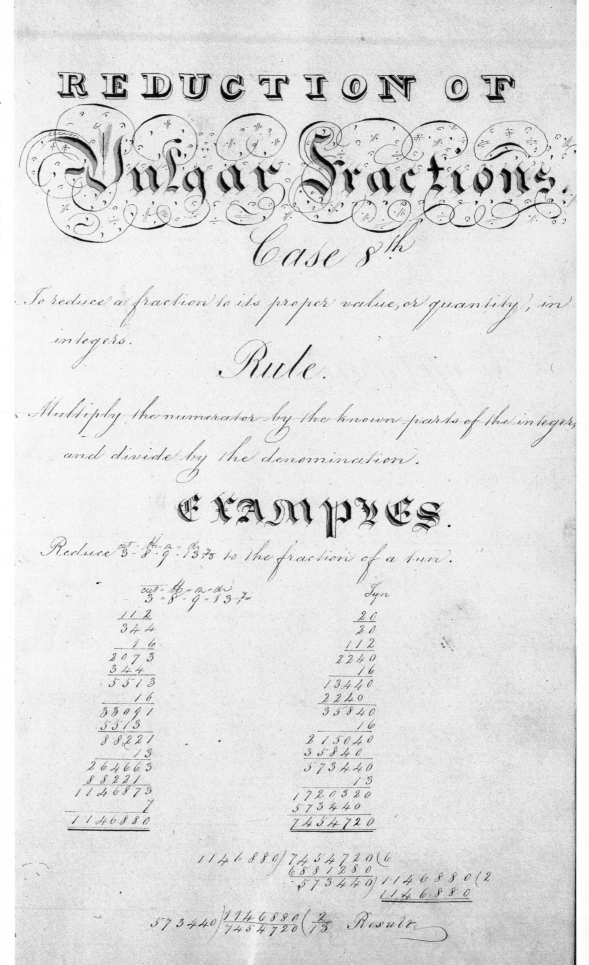

REDUCTION OF
Vulgar Fractions.

Case 8th

To reduce a fraction to its proper value, or quantity, in integers.

Rule.

Multiply the numerator by the known parts of the integer, and divide by the denomination.

EXAMPLES.

Reduce 3·8·9·137 to the fraction of a tun.

Single Rule of Three

in

VULGAR FRACTIONS.

Rule.

Prepare the given terms, if necessary, and state them as in whole numbers; multiply the second and third terms together, and divide the product by the first: Or invert the first term and mul-tiply the three together, as in Multiplication.

EXAMPLES.

If $\frac{2}{5}$ of a yard cost $\frac{7}{10}$ of a dollar what cost $\frac{3}{15}$ of a yd?

$$\frac{2}{5} \cdots \frac{3}{10} \cdots \frac{7}{15}$$

$$\frac{7}{3} \qquad \frac{13}{10}$$
$$\frac{1}{21} \qquad \frac{10}{150}$$

$$\frac{2}{5}\overline{)\frac{210}{150}}\left(\frac{105}{300}\right.$$

$$\frac{105}{100}$$
$$300\overline{)10500}$$
$$\underline{35}\text{ cts } Result$$

If $\frac{2}{3}$ of a yard cost $\frac{7}{15}$ of a pound will $\frac{3}{14}$ of a yard cost?

$$\frac{5}{3} \times \frac{7}{15} \times \frac{3}{14} = \frac{105}{630} = \text{s d Result}$$

$$630\overline{)\frac{2100}{1890}}\left(3 s\right.$$
$$\underline{210}$$

$$630\overline{)\frac{2520}{2520}}\left(4 d\right.$$

If $\frac{1}{4}$ of a yard cost $\frac{2}{3}$ of a shilling, what cost $\frac{7}{8}$ of a yd?

$$\frac{1}{4} \cdots \frac{2}{3} \cdots \frac{7}{8}$$

$$\frac{7}{14} \qquad \frac{3}{24}$$

$$\frac{1}{4}\overline{)\frac{14}{24}}\left(\frac{14}{6}\right.$$

$$6\overline{)\frac{14}{2}} = 2 \; Result$$

Single Rule of Three in Vulgar Fractions
This problem can be found in the popular book: *The Teachers Assistant, or, A System of Practical Arithmetic ... Designed to Abridge the Labour of Teachers and to Facilitate the Instruction of Youth.*. As the title suggests, the book presents several ready-made exercises that could be administered to the class by the head teacher, or by one of his/her assistants. The popularity of such books correlates with an increasing prevalence of the Lancasterian mode of education in the United States.

All the examples in this piece deal with buying and selling ribbon and cloth. Perhaps, then, this was an exercise geared to the school's female students, who learned sewing as well as "reading, writing and ciphering to the rule of three."

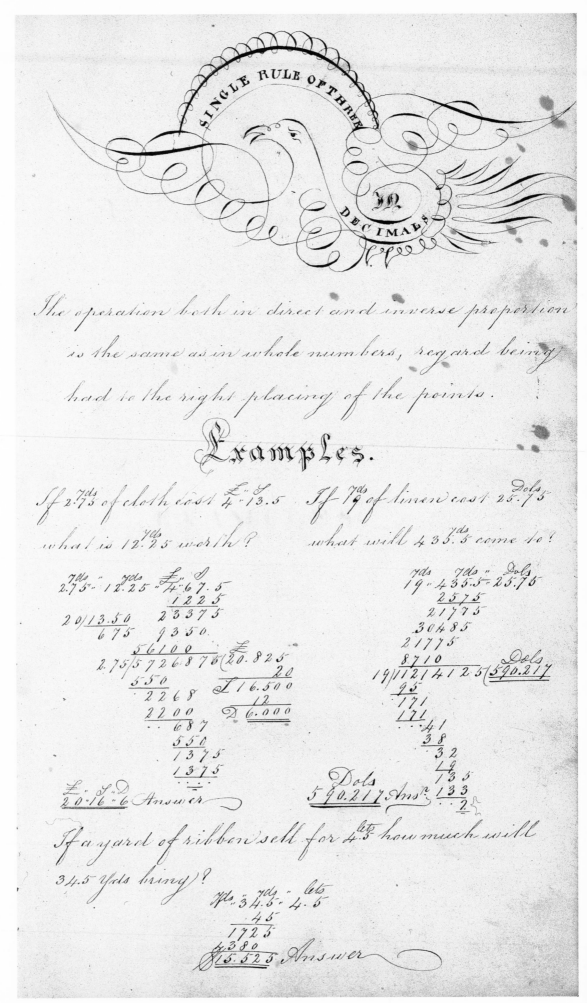

SINGLE RULE OF THREE IN DECIMALS

The operation both in direct and inverse proportion is the same as in whole numbers, regard being had to the right placing of the points.

Examples.

If 2.75 yds of cloth cost £4..13.5 what is 12.25 yds worth?

If 79 yds of linen cost 25.75 Dols what will 435.5 yds come to?

yds " yds   £..S
2.75 .. 12.25 .. 4..67.5
                 1225
20/13.50   23375
  675   9350.
       56100
2.75/5726875(20.825
     550   20
     2268   £16.500
     2200   12
      687   D 6.000
      550
     1375
     1375

£..S..D
20..16..6 Answer

yds   yds " Dols
19 " 435.5 .. 25.75
        2575
      21775
      30485
      21775
       8710   Dols
19/11214125(590.217
    95
    171
    171
     41
     38
      32
      49
      135
      133
        2

Dols
590.217 Ans.

If a yard of ribbon sell for 4.5 cts how much will 34.5 yds bring?

yds " yds " cts
yds.. 34.5 .. 4.5
        45
      1725
     1380
$15.525 Answer

48

Original Composition

BY

Andrew R Smith Aged 14 Years in the New York African Free School.

A VALEDICTORY ADRESS.

Composed and spoken at an Annual Examination, by Andrew R Smith on his leaving the school.

Respected Patrons and Friends.

With much diffidence I arise to address you on a subject which is of great importance both to myself and to those of my fellow schoolmates who are about to leave this school. I feel it my duty, on this occasion to return my humble thanks to those gentlemen who have so long been, and still are the supporters of this valuable institution.

I consider myself under many and great obligations to you, and my ardent desire and wishes are, that you may flourish and prosper in this benevolent undertaking.

To you my much respected Teacher I am greatly indebted. For your kind attention to me while under

Like valedictory addresses today, Smith's speech moves between looking back with gratitude and looking forward with hope. Yet it is important to remember that Smith was truly entering upon an unpredictable portion of his life. As New York City moved towards complete emancipation, no one was quite sure how much success free blacks would be able to achieve, or the extent to which they would be able to participate as citizens in their community.

Adeline Groves's poem, in which a black servant laments the loss of a white child, anticipates a strategy in antislavery writing that sought to create interracial networks of sympathy. That sympathy was often created through shared grief over the loss of a child.

Charles C. Andrews's *History* tells us that Adeline was no longer a student at the school when she performed this poem. As far as we know, Adeline was the only alumni to come back to present a work at an Examination Day. An account of the day can be found in Volume Two of the AFS records, where an 1821 notation describes how Adeline impressed two visitors to the school: "We then met with a young woman formerly a scholar in the school and was astonished at her talent in poetry a specimen of which she gave us." The records also indicate that there were over 300 students present at this event.

LINES

Composed by Adeline Groves, a coloured girl, formerly belonging to the N. Y. African Free School.

Dear Joseph I've surveyed this ground,
And I have walk'd this grave around,
And now, I shed the mournful tear
To leave your relics lying here.

The God, who reigns above the sky,
And bids your body here to lie,
Commands me here on earth to stay;
But soon will bear me hence away.

I'd fondly nurse thee on my arms,
And guard thee safe from every harm,
And thou should lean upon my breast,
Or on some downy pillow rest.

But God declares, this shall not be,
Indulgent home no more you'll see,
You now must slumber in this grave,
Nor could thy tender farther save.

No more you see your father's face,
Mama her son no more embrace,
On you Louisa always smiled,
And kiss'd you as her favourite child

I often gambled at your side,
My follies you would often chide,
B now these happy days are over,
Your gentle smiles are seen no more.

The Horse is a bold and fiery animal, even in a domestic state: equally intrepid as his master, he faces danger and death with ardour and magnanimity: he exults in the chase; his eyes sparkle on the course; and his whole air bespeaks spirit and energy: he is nevertheless docile and tractable; for he knows how to check and govern the vivacity and fire of his temper: he appears pleased to yield to the hand that guides him, and seems to consult the inclination of his master. He, in some measure, appears voluntarily to resign his very existence to the pleasure and accommodation of man; he delivers up his whole powers, he reserves nothing. His education commences with the loss of liberty and is finished by constraint. And such is his fidelity and attachment, when properly trained and well used, that he will die than desert his service, or disobey his commander. Who could endure to see a character, so noble, abused? Who could be guilty of such gross barbarity?

Jacob Sattin. Aged 15 Years African School 1826

This essay was likely excerpted from *Natural history, general and particular, by the Count de Buffon.* Buffon would become an important player in the emerging discipline of scientific racism, using "medical" analysis of physiological details to argue for fundamental differences between the races. The particular context of this exercise imbues Buffon's original text with new life. It is important to remember that even when children were repeating rote exercises, or copying others' examples, they brought their own experience and expectations to the lessons placed before them. Possibly, young Jacob, identified with the horse—and likely a student full of "spirit" and "energy"—may have found education itself to be a "constraint." Or perhaps, the essay's stress on the loyalty and fidelity of a being willing to subject himself to the will of a master might have struck a different chord with the son of a slave, than it would with the child of a wealthy white merchant. In fact, we can, perhaps, catch a glimpse of the student's sentiments in the essay's final two sentences, which charge those who would abuse a "character so noble" with barbarity. Those sentiments are not found in Buffon's account.

Compound Fellowship
As with many of the other math "performances," a knowledge of stock trading was considered an essential part of basic education. It also places African Free School students, at least in their imagination, as members of the prosperous merchant class who could build wealth through their own ventures, or by investing in the businesses of others.

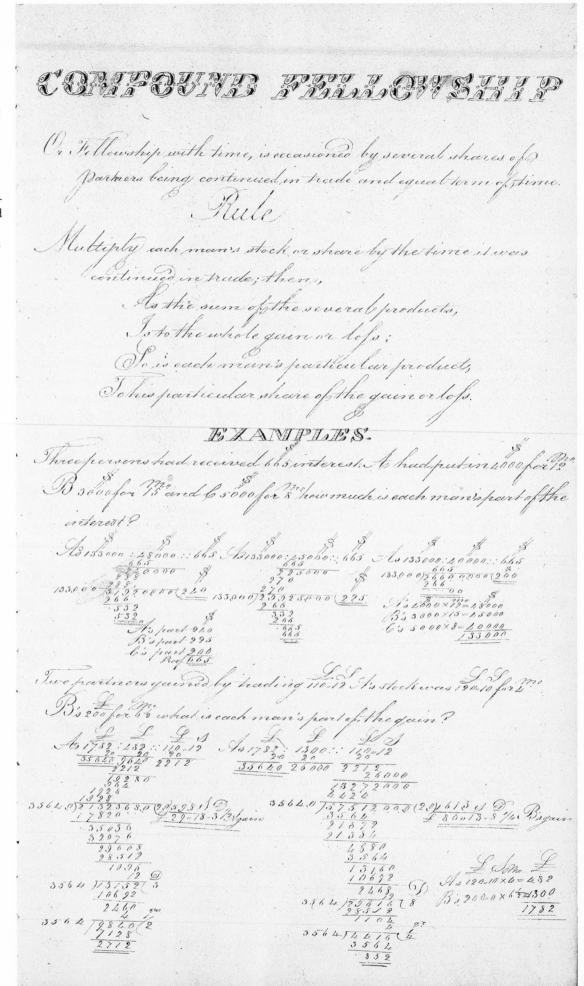

Benjamin Franklin was a stellar figure in the early republic, often considered to embody much of the young nation's primary virtues—self-reliance, resilience and ingenuity. Certainly, Ben Franklin's story of success likely proved an inspiring example to these young students, as it has to generations of Americans. This particular portrait is a copy of Charles Nicholas Cochin's famous painting of Franklin's visit to France as ambassador from 1777-85. Franklin made a point of wearing a plain brown suit and a fur cap to Paris, to portray himself as a down-to-earth American.

Dr Benjamin Franklin

was born at Boston, in New England, January 6th 1706. His integrity as a man, and his abilities as a statesman secured the most distinguished honours from the congress of the United States, and respect to his memory by the citizens of Philadelphia; where he died April 17th 1790.

Drawn by James M. Smith Aged 13 Years,
New York African School 1822

(1822)

General Lafayette visited several public schools in New York City on September 10, 1824. Lafayette was celebrated in the United States for his leading role in the American and French Revolutions. After the American Revolution, however, Lafayette was pained by the contradictions slavery posed in the new nation he had helped to create. "I would have never drawn my sword in the cause of America," he asserted, "if I had conceived that thereby I was founding a land of slavery."

It is not surprising that Lafayette was friendly with John Jay (a founding member of the New-York Manumission Society, and an advocate of the NYAFS) —both men were keenly concerned with providing training and education for slaves in order to prepare them for freedom. By 1786, Lafayette had purchased a small plantation in the French colony of Cayenne in the West Indies, where he had planned to implement a benevolent system stressing industry and education that would prepare his slaves for freedom. In 1788, he was considered such a friend to the cause of emancipation that the New-York Manumission Society elected him, along with the two famous British abolitionists Thomas Clarkson and Greenville Sharpe, honorary members of the Society.

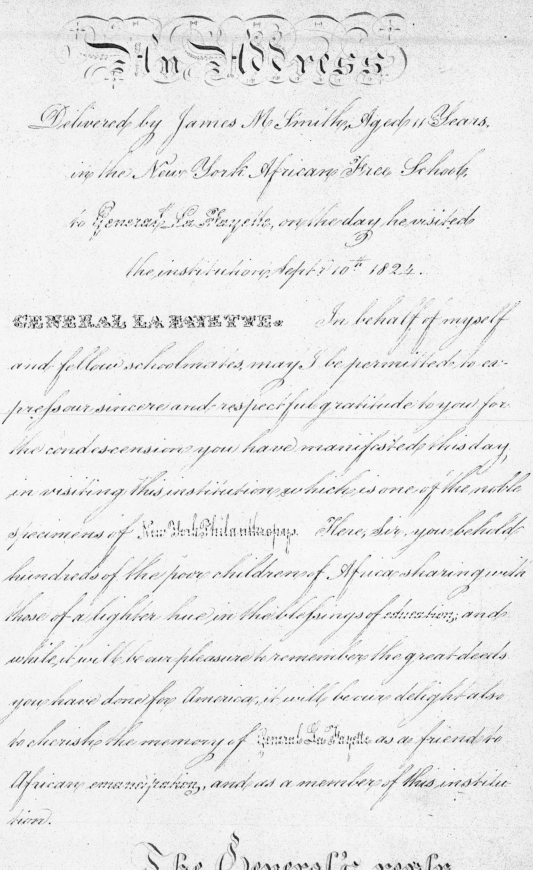

Square Root.

The wall of a fort is 24 feet in height, and a ditch of 12 feet wide surrounds the fort; I wish to know the length of a ladder that will reach from the outer edge of the ditch to the top of the wall?

The longest leg or height of the wall 24 × 24 = 576
The shortest leg or width of the ditch 12 × 12 = 144
Sum of the Squares 720

7, 20. 00, 00, (26. 83 ÷ Ans.

From the ciphering book of James McSmith Aged 13 Years

Teachers at the New York African Free School blended different learning styles in their instruction, as students used both word problems and illustrations to help them conceptualize mathematical principles.

Richard Fitch's Performance

"Of Applause," copied from John Huddlestone Wynne's *Choice Emblems,* engages in a common educational tactic of wedding moral content to artistic expression. One wonders why the instructor chose this cautionary tale for AFS students. As poor people of color in a slave nation, they faced little danger from the temptations of fame and fortune.

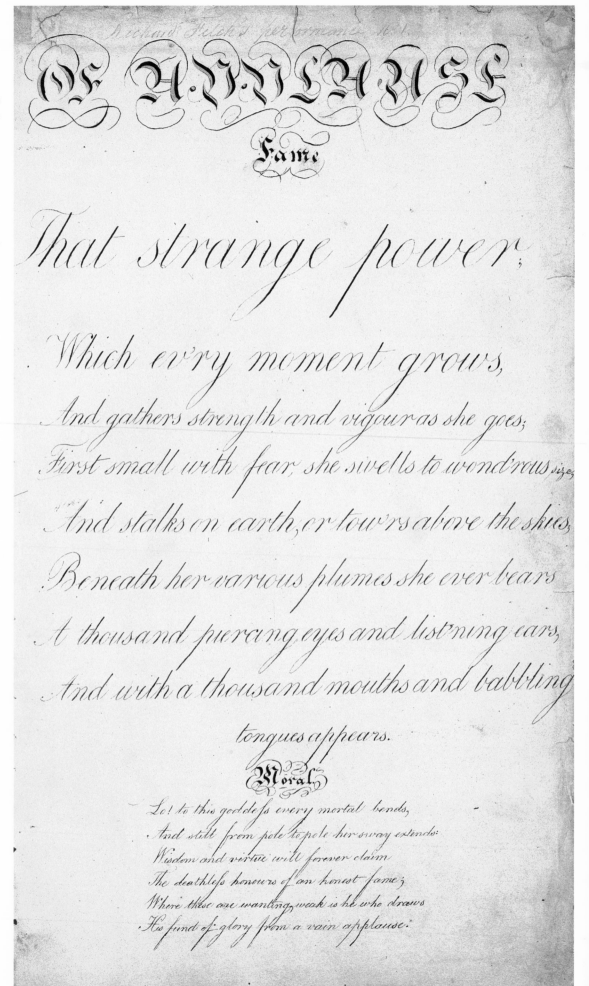

Richard Fitch's performance No 1

OF APPLAUSE

Fame

That strange power;

Which ev'ry moment grows,

And gathers strength and vigour as she goes;

First small with fear, she swells to wond'rous size,

And stalks on earth, or tow'rs above the skies;

Beneath her various plumes she ever bears

A thousand piercing eyes and listning ears,

And with a thousand mouths and babbling

tongues appears.

Moral

Lo! to this goddess every mortal bends,
And still from pole to pole her sway extends:
Wisdom and virtue will forever claim
The deathless honours of an honest fame;
Where these are wanting, weak is he who draws
His fund of glory from a vain applause.

Elements of the Graphic Arts
of Writing, Figuring, Drawing, Flourishing
Painting &c.

The Mechanical instruments to execute these
arts, is the right hand and arm, by the mo
tion of the joints of the fingers, wrist, elbow &
shoulder; in the use of a pen, pencil, brush
&c. — There are two principal motions required
viz. First, that with the fingers alone —
Secondly, that with the hand & arm. The
under tip of the little finger, being used
as a guide & regulator, and a common
Slate & slate pencil, being the most con
venient article to exercise with, & upon —

1st Exercise
Oblique Strokes, by motion of fingers
The arm from the wrist to the
Elbow being placed upon the Slate parellel
to the sides of the frame, the pencil held
between the thumb and two fore fingers, at
their full extent. Then by drawing
down the fingers, and slightly pressing
to the Slate, the pencil will make
oblique strokes, thus

//////////////

But in bringing back the fingers to the
first position, an upward stroke may
be made, without lifting the pencil from
the slate, thus

////////___//////___//////////

Ironically, these instructions
on teaching the graphic arts
represent the only example
of poor penmanship in the
volume! It is likely that
these pages were not pre-
sented formally, and
instead, represent a nineteenth-century "lesson
plan." The instructions
move through six lessons,
progressing in difficulty.
Penmanship, drawing,
figuring, and "flourishing"
are all seen as part of a con-
tinuum, and are given equal
weight. We can also sympa-
thize with left-handed
pupils, who must have had
a difficult time working
under the assertion, stated
on page 31, that "the
mechanical instrument to
execute these [graphic] arts
is the right hand and arm."

4th Lesson
Exercise in Writing — By motion of fingers

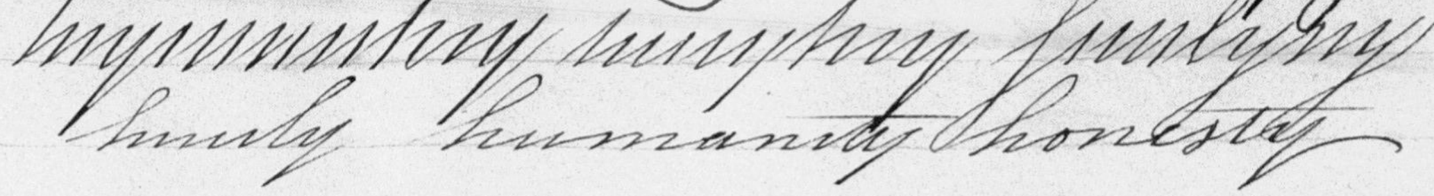

(penmanship exercise strokes) humanity honesty

5th Lesson
Exercises by motion of Hand & Arm
Axis of motion oblique

(penmanship exercise strokes)

Axis of motion Horizontal

(penmanship exercise strokes)

6th Lesson.
The Four Rolling Motion — Axis Horizontal

(penmanship exercise with loops)

False

1   2
3   4

Napoleon Francois, Charles Joseph, Drawn by James McCune Smith, Aged 12 years, New York African Free School

Napoleon II had been legally named as the successor to Napoleon by a legislative body upon Napoleon I's abdication. He fled, with his mother, at the age of four to Austria, where he was eventually named the Duke of Reichstadt. In Austria, his French tutors were replaced by German-speaking instructors, in an attempt to erase his connections with his troublesome history. Historical documents indicate that the young Napoleon would ask repeatedly about his father, and was never given a satisfactory answer. One wonders how young black students, who may well have had their own family histories stolen from them through slavery, might have felt about this young, dispossessed prince, exiled far from his native land.

Because much of the education the male students received stressed nautical skills, geography, drawing, and cartography were important fields of study. Knowledge of seaports along the Atlantic shore would have been especially useful, as recent historical studies have noted a striking rise in the number of black men employed in seafaring occupations between 1740-1820. By 1803, roughly eighteen percent of all seafaring jobs were held by black men.

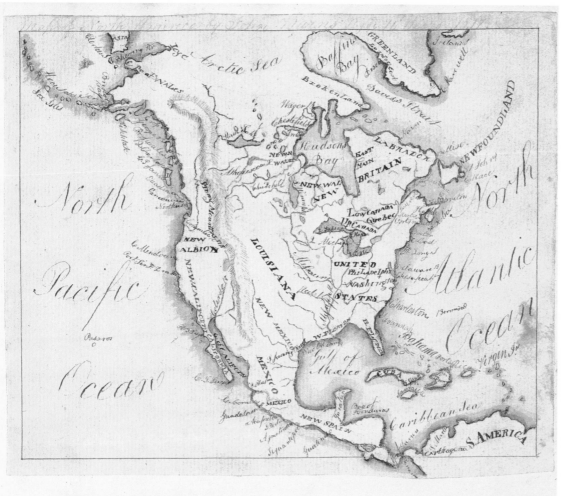

Edward Hains' Second attempt May 1819.

Aged 14 Years.

Top image: Unlike many of the images in this volume, this map is explicitly described in an outside source. Charles C. Andrews, the school's principal for over twenty years, was particularly proud of this map, or one like it. He gave it to the newspaper *The Commercial Advertiser,* which describes the events of an examination day, and notes "a map of the United States, drawn and lettered (as we are assured by Mr. Andrews) by a lad ten years old." The newspaper then adds that "[i]t can be examined in this office," which seems to invite the public to test the validity of the claim, and to join in admiration of the student's work.

Bottom image: As the attribution "second attempt" indicates, students would often make more than one copy of a particular piece in the effort to perfect their work. Landscape painting, an outgrowth of the Romantic movement, was an important force in British art in the eighteenth and early nineteenth century. Within ten years of this sketch, American artists would work to make the landscape genre their own, as the Hudson River School (which, in part, celebrated the beautiful countryside along New York's Hudson River) began to emerge in the 1820s. One of the innovators of this school, Thomas Cole, created the National Academy of Design in New York City. While we cannot tell if this image is of a European scene, or an American vista, it does seem significant that it does not showcase any of the castles or gothic ruins so popular in European landscapes of the era.

The headdress, gentle curls, and classic features were all indicative of current models of beauty in the eighteenth and nineteenth century. As in so many areas of their education, New York African Free School students' art lessons about beauty and grace were based on white European traditions and models. Nowhere in this volume do we find a portrait of a black subject.

Drawn by Andrew R Smith Aged 14 Years 1822.
New York African Free School.

A pastoral scene drawn by valedictorian Andrew R. Smith. Little is known of the life of this talented student following his years at the New York African Free School.

Drawn by Andrew R Smith Aged 14 Years 1822.
New York African Free School.

Top image: This sketch, like many of the other pieces of artwork featured in this volume focuses on a rural scene. Rather than a pastoral subject from the distant past, however, this sketch features touches of the modern, including a steamboat.

Bottom page: Ship This picture, likely of a contemporary battleship called a man-of-war, falls squarely within the genre of nautical art that was in vogue throughout the late eighteenth and early nineteenth centuries. Drawing was considered essential for people who were planning nautical careers: it provided another way of using spatial skills, and would prepare sailors to visually record the sights and scenes of their travels. Boys at the New York African Free School spent a good deal of time learning navigation and other skills suited for a maritime careers, which was one of the few venues open to free black men at the time. One of the school's most famous alumni, radical abolitionist Henry Highland Garnet, earned a living for a while on a Cuba-bound ship.

The rose nestled in thorns was a popular emblem found in many educational books.

Although there is no text accompanying this particular piece, poetry accompanying similar illustrations often suggested that pleasure and pain were mixed, and that beauty was transitory.

Camel

Like the lion, the camel represented exotic locales for New York students. Its prominence in biblical stories and iconography would have made it a strong candidate for inclusion in drawing lessons.

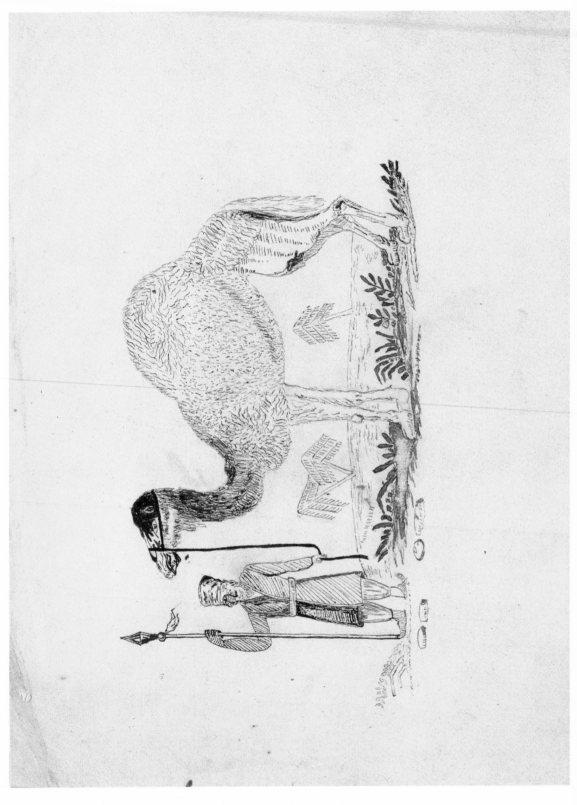

A man returning from a hunt was a central theme in rural European art that was associated with pastoral leisure and pleasure. However, when translated through NYAFS students' sensibility, the subject might have created a different set of associations altogether. Imagine what some young black students at the school—Henry Highland Garnet, for example—might have thought while completing this drawing exercise. Garnet, who went on to become a radical abolitionist, escaped from slavery with his family, and would have been all too familiar with the figure of a white man using dogs to track runaway slaves.

Many of the drawing books of the era asked students to focus on pieces of larger images in order to master the small details.

Top image: This carefully rendered sketch falls within the style of rural art made popular by Thomas Gainsborough, who often created images focusing on humble cottages. These rural paintings revealed a shift in emphasis from the stately mansions and stiff portraiture of the upper classes, to a celebration of the rustic activities and plain dwellings of the nation's poor.

Bottom image: This is a representation of the great seal of the United States, which was the product of a collaborative effort by founding fathers beginning on July 4, 1776 and finalized six years later on June 20, 1782. During the 1820s New York City's blacks often highlighted their American character in an effort to counter the American Colonization Society and its plans to send free people of color back to Africa.

Drawing exercises often asked students to create portraits that embodied certain emotions or states of mind. This process taught students to pay close attention to the body language of others (What does a man do with his eyebrows when he is angry? How do one's eyes crinkle when one is surprised?) This portrait is clearly influenced by classical sources: the man is drawn with Roman features and dress.

Innocence

Thomas Lattin Aged 13 Years. 1826. New York.

December 2nd 1812, M. Burns. Drawing masters often asked students to "try on" different facial expressions. Note the curled lip, then, as now, associated with a pretentious, disdainful attitude. There was great emphasis in the educational material of the era on the correlation between body language, mood and emotion.

Contempt.
Painted By M. Burns
Dec.r 2d 1812

This intriguing picture rais-
es a number of possibilities,
as we have very little information to help us discover
what or where this building
is. The caption below reads
"New York African Free
School," but students place
this attribution at the bottom of many of the images
in this volume, so it does
not necessarily denote the
name of the building itself.
Perhaps, however, this is a
rendering of the first building to house the school. We
do know a New York
African Free Schoolhouse
existed on Cliff-Street, and
burned down in an 1814 fire
that also consumed St.
George's Chapel. It is also
possible that this image
depicts not a contemporary
American scene, but rather,
a copy of a rural cottage
painting in the manner of
European artists like
Gainsborough.

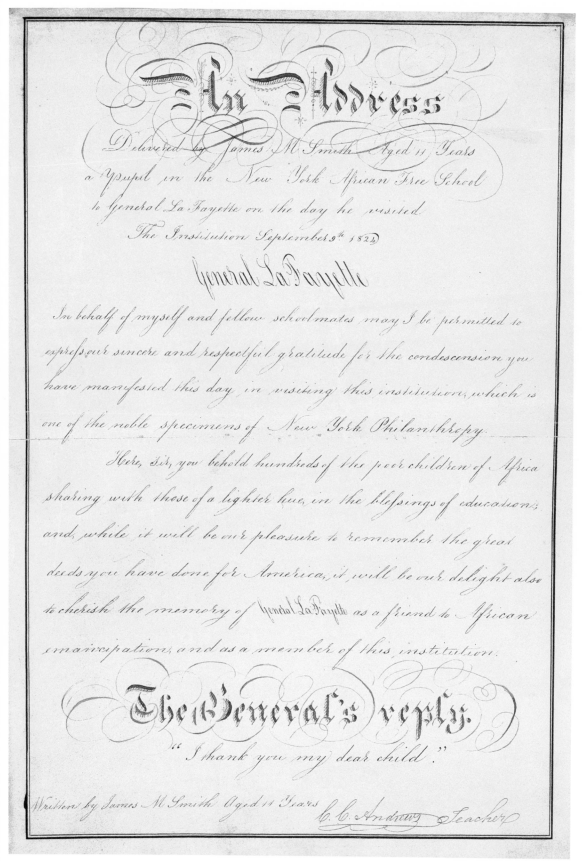

An Address

Delivered by James M Smith Aged 11 Years

a Pupil in the New York African Free School

to General La Fayette on the day he visited

The Institution September 9th 1824

General La Fayette

In behalf of myself and fellow school-mates may I be permitted to

express our sincere and respectful gratitude for the condescension you

have manifested this day in visiting this institution, which is

one of the noble specimens of New York Philanthropy.

Here, Sir, you behold hundreds of the poor children of Africa

sharing with those of a lighter hue, in the blessings of education;

and, while it will be our pleasure to remember the great

deeds you have done for America, it, will be our delight also

to cherish the memory of General La Fayette as a friend to African

emancipation, and as a member of this institution.

The General's reply.

" I thank you my dear child."

Written by James M Smith Aged 11 Years   C. C. Andrews   Teacher

The replication and inclusion of several copies of this address reveal what an important moment it was for the African Free School. Note that in this version, we learn that the address was authored by James McCune Smith. The earlier version gives no such attribution. We also have the signature of the schoolmaster, Charles C. Andrews, whose presence looms large throughout the Examination Day records.

An Address

Delivered by James M Smith
a Pupil in the New York African Free School
to General LaFayette on the day he visited
the institution Septr. 9th 1824

General La Fayette   In behalf of myself and fellow schoolmates

may I be permitted to express our sincere and respectful grati-

tude for the condescension you have manifested this day in

visiting this institution which is one of the noble specimens of

New York Philanthropy.   Here, sir, you behold hundreds

of the poor children of Africa sharing with those of a lighter

hue in the blessings of education; and while it will be our

pleasure to remember the great deeds you have done for America,

it will be our delight also to cherish the memory of General La Fayette as a

friend to African emancipation, and as a member of this institution.

The General's reply.

Selected Transcriptions

PAGE 1: *Henry Hill's Performance*

Emblem of Education
See in what Evil plight yon vine appears
Nor spreading leaves, nor purple clusters bears,
But if around the elm her arm she throws,
Or by some friendly prop supported grows,
Soon shall the stem be clad with foliage green,
And cluster'd grapes beneath the leaves be seen.

Moral

Thus prudent care must rear the youthful mind,
By love supported, and with toil refin'd
'Tis thus alone the human plant can rise;
Unprop'd, it droops, and unsupported dies.

PAGE 5: *Of Necessary Confidence, Hope is the First great blessing*

Here below:
The only balm to heal corroding wo[e],
It is the staff of age, the sick man's health;
The prisoner's freedom, and the poor man's Wealth
The sailor's safety: tasting as our breath,
It still holds nor quits us e'en in death

Moral:

Encourage hope, which heals all human care; the last mad folly is a sad despair.

If you are wise, that dreadful evil shun, nor fall unpitied, by yourself undone.

PAGE 8: UNHAPPY CLOSE OF LIFE

How shocking must they summons be, O death
To him that is at ease in his possessions!
Who counting on long years of pleasure here,
Is quite unfinished for the world to come!

IN THAT DREAD MOMENT

How the frantic soul
Roams round the walls of her clay tenement;
Runs to each avenue, and shrieks for help;
But shrieks in vain! How wistfully she looks
On all she's leaving, now no longer hers!
A little longer; yet a little longer;
O might she stay to wash away her stains;
And fit her for her passage

MOURNFUL SIGHT

Her very eyes weep blood; and ev'ry groan
She heaves is big with horror. But the foe,
Like a staunch murd'rer steady to his purpose,
Pursues her close, thro' ev'ry lane of life;
Nor misses once the track, but presses on,
Till, forc'd at last to the tremendous verge,
At last she sinks to

EVERLASTING RUIN

Edward Haines
New York
February 1819

PAGE 12: *Oh Liberty Thou Pow'r*

Supremely bright,
Profuse of bliss, and pregnant with delight
Perpetual pleasures in thy presence reign;
And smiling plenty leads thy wanton train.
Eas'd of her load, subjection grows more light;

AND POVERTY LOOKS CHEERFUL

In thy sight
Though make's the gloomy face of nture gay;
Givs't beauty to the sun, and pleasure to the day

PAGE 13 & 14: *Fellowship*

Fellowship is a rule by which merchants etc. trading in company with a joint stock are enabled to ascertain each person's particular share of the gain or loss, in proportion to his share in the joint stock.
By this rule also legacies are adjusted, and the effects of bankrupts are divided etc.

Case 1st

When several stocks in company are considered without regard to time.

Rule

As the whole sum, or stock
Is to the whole gain or loss,
So is each person's share in the stock, etc.
To his share of the gain or loss

Proof

The sum of the several shares must equal the gain or loss.

PAGE 14: *Fellowship, Cont'd*

EXAMPLES

The merchants, trading together, gained $800. As stock was 1200 Dollars,
B's 800 Dollars and C's 2000 Dollars: what was each man's share of the gain?

PAGE 15: *A Short account of the Lion*

This animal is produced in Africa, and the hottest parts of Asia. It is found in the greatest numbers in the scorched and desolate regions of the torrid zone, in the deserts of Sahara and Biledulgerid, and in all the interior parts of the vast continent of Africa. For these desert regions from whence mankind are driven by the rigorous heat of the climate, this animal reigns sole master: His disposition seems to partake of the ardour of its native soil. Inflamed by the influence of a burning sun, its rage is most horrendous, and its courage undaunted.

The form of the lion is strikingly bold and majestic. His large and shaggy mane, which he can erect at his pleasure, surrounding his awful front; his huge eyebrows, his round and fiery eyeballs, which upon the least irritation, seems to glow with peculiar luster, together with the formidable appearance of his teeth, exhibit a picture of terrific grandeur which no words can describe.

PAGE 16: *On the Lion*

The Lion is a noble creature,
And has a strong terrifick feature;
This roaring which is loud as thunder, Strikes all around
with fear and wonder.

On Afric's dark and sultry shore,
This mighty beast is heard to roar,
And oft on dry and barren grounds,
He most majestically stands.

He prowls and roams about at night,
And travelers tremble, all with fright;
They dare not turn about to fly,
Thinking that he is very nigh.

He roams the desert far and wide,
His faithful dam close by his side;
The strongest beast they will attack
And with their paw will break their back

PAGE 17: *On the Fair*

The work of children here you find,
The fruit of labour, and of mind;
The month is pat, the day is come,
And he that gaines [sic] shall have the sum

Although our minds are weak and feeble,
Some can use a knife or needle;
If fortune by my side will stand,
I mean to join the happy band

A girl can make a frock or coat,
A boy a pretty little boat;
Another girl a pretty quilt,
A handsome cap, or gown of silk.

To excel we all will work and strive,
Till to perfection we arrive;
Many will work and strive in vain,
The fifty tickets to obtain

Our little fair to us is great,
As any other in the state;
It is a cheerful time to some,
Though idle scholars will not come.

The child that comes to this good school
Should never rest an idle fool;
Though there were many once were so,
We find them daily wiser grow.

PAGE 18: *On the Fair, Cont'd*

The beauties of our little fair,
You will not know if your'e [sic] not there
It will be taking too much time
To enter all the things in rhyme,

P.S. You'll find mistakes I do not doubt,
And if you do please leave them out.

Andrew R. Smith

Explanation

It will here be necessary to explain what is meant by the fair which occasioned the above lines. Our Teacher thinking it useful to encourage an emulation amongst us, proposed to reward every scholar who should produce on the 1st Monday in every month, a specimen of his or her ingenuity in mechanics, needle work, drawing, Composition, either in prose or poetry &c. Many of us tried hard to gain the highest prize (50 School Tickets)

The above being considered as deserving it procured for the writer, not only the highest prize, but also the commendation of his preceptor.

PAGES 22 & 23: *A Valedictory Address*
Original Composition by Andrew R. Smith, Aged 14 Years in the New York African Free School.

A Valedictory Address

Respected Patrons and Friends,

With much diffidence, I arise to address you on a subject which is of great importance, both to myself and to those of my fellow schoolmates who are about to leave the school. I feel it my duty, on this occasion to return my humble thanks to those gentlemen who have so long been and still are the supporters of this valuable institution.

I consider myself under many great obligations to you, and my ardent desire and wishes are, that you may flourish and prosper in this benevolent undertaking.

To you, my much respected teacher, I am greatly indebted. For your kind attention to me while under your care, I most sincerely and humbly thank you.

When I first became your pupil, I was ignorant of letters, and learned my A, B, C, by means of writing in thousand: since that time, I have passed regularly through every class in the school and have had the honor of filling almost every office in the same, and more than this, down to the present day, have had the pleasure to enjoy the expressions of approbation of my teacher.

My books, and exercises, exhibited before you this day, will, I doubt not, be regarded by you gentlemen who are trustees of this school, as testimonials in my favor that your labor and that of my preceptor have not been bestowed on me in vain.

As the various exercises of the day have detained you some time, it requires me to be short: in conclusion, let me remind you my fellow Schoolmates, who are about to leave with me, that we are now entering into a wild field, and that we must be industrious and upright to make respectable members of society, and to be an honor to our parents; We must make such use of our learning as will prove a blessing to ourselves, and to the community with which Providence now calls us to mix.

PAGE 24: *Lines Composed by Adeline Groves, a coloured girl, formerly belonging to the N.Y. African Free School*

Dear Joseph I've survey'd this ground,
And I have walk'd this grave around;
And now I shed the mournful tear,

To leave your relics lying here.
The God, who reigns above the sky,
And bids your body here to lie,
Commands me here on earth to stay;
But soon will bear me hence away.
I'd fondly nurse thee in my arms,
And guard thee safe from every harm
And thou should lean upon my breast,
Or on some downy pillow rest.
But God declares, this shall not be,
Indulgent home no more you'll see,
You now must slumber in this grave,
Nor could thy tender father save
No more you see your father's face,
Mama her son no more embrace
On you Louisa always smiled
And kiss'd you as her favourite child.
I often gamboll'd at your side,
My follies you would often chide,
But now those happy days are over,
Your gentle smiles are seen no more.

PAGE 25: *Horse essay—Jacob Pattin, Aged 15 years, African School 1826.*

The Horse is a bold and fiery animal, even in a domestic state: equally intrepid as his master, he faces danger and death with ardour and magnanimity: he exults in the chase; his eyes sparkle on the course, and his whole air bespeaks spirit and energy: he is nevertheless docile and tractable; for he knows how to check and govern the vivacity and fire of his temper: he appears pleased to yield to the hand that guides him, and seems to consult the inclination of his master He, in some measure, appears voluntarily to resign his very existence to the pleasure and accommodation of man; he delivers his whole powers, he reserves nothing. His education commences with the loss of liberty and his finished by constraint. And such is his fidelity and attachment when properly trained and well used, that he will die [rather] than desert his service, or disobey his commander. Who could endure to see a character, so noble, abused? Who could be guilty of such barbarity?

PAGE 28: *An Address Delivered by James M. Smith, Aged 11 years, in the New York African Free School, to General Lafayette, on the day he visited the institution Sept 10th, 1824*

General Lafayette. In behalf of myself and fellow schoolmates, may I be permitted to express our sincere and respectful gratitude to you for the condescension you have manifested this day, in visiting this institution, which is one of the noble specimens of New York Philanthropy. Here, Sir, you behold hundreds of the poor children of Africa sharing with those of a lighter hue, in the blessings of education, and while, it will be our pleasure to remember the great deeds you have done for America, it will be our delight also to cherish the memory of General La Fayette as a friend to African emancipation, and as a member of this institution.

The General's reply:
"Thank you, my dear child"

PAGE 30: *Of Applause*
Fame
This strange power
Which every moment grows,
And gathers strength and vigour as she goes;
First small with fear, she swells to wondrous size,
And stalks on earth, or towrs above the skies,
Beneath her various plumes she ever bears
A thousand piercing eyes and listening ears,
And with a thousand mouths and babbling tongues appears.
Moral
Lo! to this goddess every mortal bends,
And still from pole to pole her sway extends:
Wisdom and virtue will forever claim
The deathless honours of an honest fame;
When these are wanting, weak is he who draws
His fund of glory from a rain of applause.

Selections for Further Reading

BIBLIOGRAPHY

Andrews, Charles C. *The History of the New York African Free School*, (rpr.1830; New York: Arno Press, 1969)

Berlin, Ira, and Leslie M. Harris, eds. *Slavery in New York*. New York: New Press, 2005.

Gellman, David N., and David Quigley, eds. *Jim Crow New York: A Documentary History of Race and Citizenship, 1777-1787*. New York: New York University Press, 2003.

Harris, Leslie M. *In the Shadow of Slavery: African Americans in New York City. 1626-1863*. Chicago, IL: University of Chicago Press, 2003.

Hodges, Graham Russell. *Root & Branch: African Americans in New York and East Jersey, 1613-1863*. Chapel Hill: University of North Carolina Press, 1999.

White, Shane. *Somewhat More Independent: The End of Slavery in New York City, 1770- 1810*. Athens, GA: University of George Press, 1990.

White, Shane. *Stories of Freedom in Black New York*. Cambridge, MA: Harvard University Press, 2002.

MULTIMEDIA RESOURCES

New-York Historical Society. *Hidden Sites of Slavery and Freedom: A Walking Tour of New York City*: http://touchtonetours.com/nyh/

New York State Council for the Social Studies. *New York and Slavery: Complicity and Resistance*. http://nyscss.org/resources/publications/NyandSlavery.cfm

Potts, Ian, producer. *Slave Island: New York's Hidden History*. Princeton, NJ: Films for the Humanities & Sciences, 2004.

Set in Galliard type. Printed by the Studley Press. Designed by Jerry Kelly.